Dawn of the Final Caliphate

Dedication

This book is dedicated to all of those brave brothers and sisters within Islam, who boldly defy the preachers of hate, and the advocates of martial brutality. Their genuine desire for a modern Islamic Reformation can only lead to peace and harmony with all of those who do not share their faith.

DAWN OF THE
FINAL CALIPHATE

———⊷⟨ତ⟩⊷———

James Hadfield-Hyde

Bernini Publishing

First published in the United Kingdom in 2018 by
Bernini Publishing

ISBN 978-0-9572770-4-5 paperback
ISBN 978-0-9572770-3-8 hardback

CONTENTS

—◦◦◦—

ABOUT THE AUTHOR

———∘⦿∘———

James Hadfield-Hyde was born in England in 1949. He was privately educated at boarding school, and then went on to further his education in the United States of America. His devout Roman Catholic upbringing aroused the curiosity in him to explore other religions. James travelled extensively throughout North Africa, and the Middle East, where he developed a keen interest in Moorish architecture and the history of Islam. He became a Conservative political activist as early as 1970, when he campaigned alongside Anthony Barber MP, the then Chancellor of the Exchequer. Remaining a highly active supporter of the Conservative Party until 2012, he joined the United Kingdom Independence Party in defiance of Prime Minister David Cameron's stance on Europe. As a dedicated Brexiteer, he toured the country giving speeches and participating in public debates. Although now retired, and living mostly abroad, during his long career, he has been a property developer, a dealer in fine arts and antiques, a television broadcaster, an advertising agency writer, an award winning playwright, an inventor, a factory owner, an author, and an Ostrich farmer.

FOREWORD

by Neil Hamilton AM

———❦———

A
ccording to the Muslim calendar, the year is 1439. In AD 1439, Christians were burning heretics and inflicting other appalling punishments for refusal to conform to the prevailing religion. The disturbing feature of 21st century Islam is that so many Muslims worldwide are stuck in a similar mediaeval mindset.

When I was a boy in 1950s Britain, Mohamedans (as we then called them) were a numerically insignificant minority. The only mosque of which I was aware was the exotic oriental building at Woking, visible from the Portsmouth to Waterloo train.

As recently as 1961, there were only 50,000 Muslims across England and Wales. By 2014, the number had exploded to over 3,000,000 or 5.4% of the total population. Islam is the fastest growing religious confession in the UK and its adherents have the lowest average age of all major religious groups. Between 2001 and 2009 the Muslim population increased almost 10 times faster than the non-Muslim population.

By 2050, Muslims will nearly equal the number of Christians around the world, driven primarily by differences in fertility rates and the size of youth populations among the world's major religions. From 200 million worldwide in 1900, the

Muslim population increased to 551 million in 1970 and tripled again to 1.6 billion by 2010. In 2050, the number is forecast to be 2.75 billion.

Islam is a militant faith commanding total obedience from the faithful in all walks of life. By contrast, the mainstream Christian denominations have long since ceased to be "the church militant." The C of E is now more like "the church hesitant" and the 10 Commandments relegated to "the 10 Suggestions." Political correctness has debilitated it into virtual irrelevance – more people visit the local bottle bank on Sunday to worship at the shrine of the new religion of "recycling," which has developed its own rituals of bin-observance, with strict fines for non-compliance.

What a contrast with the confident, expanding, proselytizing faith of Islam. Muslims believe that Islam is the complete and universal version of a primordial faith revealed many times before through prophets including Adam, Abraham, Moses and Jesus. They believe that the Quran is the unaltered and final revelation of God and the very word "Islam" indicates its claim to subordinate all secular endeavour to the requirements of the faith. In the religious context, "Islam" means "voluntary submission to God."

In the last 50 years, Britain has been transformed by mass immigration into a multi-cultural society. Fewer than half of London residents were born in the UK. Unfortunately, this does not mean a society transformed by integration into a new cohesiveness. The large English cities are a series of monocultures living separately side-by-side, with "white flight" having largely emptied them of the "indigenous" population.

Just as startling is the religious transformation of Britain. 12% of London's population is now Muslim. In the London Borough of Tower Hamlets it is 36% and Newham 24%. Outside London, in Blackburn it is 19%, Bradford 16%, Waltham Forest 15%, Luton 15% and Birmingham 15%. This population will grow at a disproportionate rate, as 9.5% of all UK children under five years old have Muslim parents.

James Hadfield Hyde's book is a reminder of the scale of the challenge which this poses. The vast majority of Muslims are not, of course, foaming-at-the-mouth radicals and pose no threat of violence or to "British values." But, with such a large Muslim population and continued mass immigration, a very small minority of religious extremists can create havoc.

In 2016, Channel 4 commissioned a survey of the social attitudes of British Muslims. The results are very worrying.

The former Chairman of the Equality and Human Rights Commission, Trevor Phillips, was asked to analyse and interpret the survey for a TV documentary. Phillips argued that the survey's findings pose profound questions for our society, with implications for future relations between Britain's Muslim and non-Muslim communities.

> He said: "Hearing what British Muslims themselves think, rather than listening to those purporting to speak on their behalf, is critical if we are to prevent the establishment of a nation within our nation. Many of the results will be troubling to Muslims and non-Muslims alike – and the analysis of the age profile shows us that the social attitudes revealed are unlikely to change quickly.

"The integration of Britain's Muslims will probably be the hardest task we've ever faced. It will require the abandonment of the milk-and-water multiculturalism still so beloved of many, and the adoption of a far more muscular approach to integration."

"A chasm exists between those Muslims surveyed and the wider population on attitudes to liberal values on issues such as gender equality, homosexuality and issues relating to freedom of expression. And it also reveals significant differences on attitudes to violence and terrorism."

The survey's findings include:

Only 34% would inform the police if they thought somebody they knew was getting involved with people who support terrorism in Syria

4% sympathise with people who take part in suicide bombings

4% sympathise with people who commit terrorist actions as a form of political protest.

52% do not believe that homosexuality should be legal in Britain

47% do not believe that it is acceptable for a school teacher to be homosexual

23% support the introduction of Sharia Law.

32% refuse to condemn those who take part in violence against those who mock the Prophet

39% agree "wives should always obey their husbands".

31% refuse to completely condemn those who take part in stoning those who commit adultery.

31% think it's acceptable for a man to have more than one wife

All this quite clearly poses fundamental challenges to modern Britain, which we ignore at our peril. We must understand the faith and history of Islam if we are to find solutions. James Hadfield-Hyde's book is a timely and readable starting-point.

Neil Hamilton is a member of the National Assembly for Wales and Leader of the United Kingdom Independence Party, Wales. He is a former Conservative Party member of the British Parliament (1983 – 1997) and was the Under Secretary of State for Corporate Affairs (1992 – 1994) in the government of Prime Minister, John Major. He is a Barrister by profession.

Chapter 1

MY AWAKENING TO THE WORLD OF ISLAM

─·◦⊙◦·─

It is not my intent to offer this work as a serious academic study of Islam and its mindset; I leave that task to the likes of Dr. Sebastian Gorka and Douglas Murray. However, I felt that there was a need to explain in simple terms, hopefully without bias or distortion, the historical facts relating to the effects Islam is having on our world today and what we can do about it.

My first encounter with the intolerance of Islam came in 1976. I was in my mid-to-late twenties. Along with Sue, my girlfriend at the time, we had decided that we should take an impromptu trip to Morocco. One has to bear in mind that we were still living in the days of the "Hippies" and the "Flower Power" movement, and Morocco, particularly Marrakesh, was one of those really 'cool' places to go to. I can honestly say that neither Sue nor I were remotely Hippie. She was an astute, successful young businesswoman who always drove the latest Porsche motor car, and I was the epitomised product of the English boarding school system. Nonetheless, we were of that generation. Shortly after arriving, I found myself lying on my back in a mud hut suffering with dysentery and pleading with Sue that I didn't want to die in Africa. But, we were young and resilient and within three days I was back on my feet and heading up into the High

1

Atlas mountains. I can't quite remember how, but somewhere along our travels we met up with a lovely Australian girl who decided to tag along with us. The very thought of any parent allowing their daughter to travel alone in a remote part of North Africa in this day and age doesn't bear thinking about. We lived in a different world back then in 1976, and exotic lands were still an adventure playground. An average English person's insight into the Islamic world was based on little more than Peter O'Toole's enactment as T. E. Lawrence in the 1962 film *Lawrence of Arabia*. Omar Sharif was the heart-throb for most Western women at the time and Alec Guinness, who played the part of Prince Feisal, appeared wise and kindly. The reality differs somewhat.

Perched precariously high on the side of a mountain was the focus of our determined effort to meet and befriend the locals. It was a village of flat-roofed houses, principally made with mud and handmade bricks. After a steep climb of a couple of miles in the blazing heat, we were eventually warmly greeted by a young boy called Mohammed. With a mixture of pidgin English, schoolboy French, a little Spanish, and an assortment of hand gestures, we made ourselves understood, and the young fellow invited us to meet his mother and to show us his home. He was most proud of the fact that his was the only house in the village with two levels leading up onto the roof.

We respectfully removed our shoes and stepped inside.

The mother was politely subservient in manner and she kindly offered us the refreshment of mint tea. I remember we all had to sit round on the floor as the house was completely devoid of any furniture. There was an array of rolled-up woven mats stacked nearby, which Mohammed explained were their night-time beds. In the corner of the room was a mud oven with a charcoal fire burning beneath it. Live rabbits were incarcerated in a hole in the wall, where, from behind wooden bars, they could view their relatives being butchered and prepared for the pot. We were shown up on to the rooftop to admire the spectacular view and, at the risk of outstaying our welcome, we decided to leave soon afterwards. It bewildered me that after occupying the same lands for thousands of years, they were still choosing to live without making any effort to improve on the most basic of comforts or hygiene. Had I stepped over their threshold as a soldier in the army of Caesar Augustus, I would have been greeted by the identical domestic scene. If the Romans couldn't get them to modernise, who could?

We graciously thanked our hosts and I offered the woman a selection of dirham coins, which she gratefully accepted. Outside, we rearranged ourselves and prepared for further exploration of the place, but that was when things suddenly changed.

We found ourselves confronted by a group of about ten men, who gathered round and silently stared at us. As the silence prevailed there was a trickle of all ages to appear on the scene from out of each of the houses – all men and boys, no women. Foremost was what was obviously the village elder, or imam. He was an ancient man with a long white chinstrap beard and his cragged face was blackened by the ravages of time. We offered them smiles and friendly gestures, but got a cold blank response in return.

The imam broke the silence and started shouting at us in Arabic. We hadn't the foggiest idea what he was saying, but whatever it was, it definitely wasn't cordial. We started to fear that we were in serious trouble, and there was no one there to protect us. We began to make feeble apologies to them in English. The old man bent down and picked up a rock; he held it in his hand for several seconds as he continued to shout abuse. Then, he threw it at us. That opened a floodgate of frenzy as all the men started to find stones and began hurling them at us, one after the other. The three of us took off like the wind with the entire village of men in hot pursuit, screaming vengeance. After a mile or so, the chase finally dwindled and the men returned home.

None of us were seriously hurt, but it was a terrifying experience nonetheless. We knew full well that had we failed to outrun them, or taken a wrong turning into a cul-de-sac, then, without question, the end result would have led to all of our deaths. Knowing what we know now, they would have only killed the two girls after having passed them round and gang-raped them first. I had just experienced my very first collision with the alien world of Islam.

We were completely baffled as to why they had been so hostile towards us for no apparent reason, when Mohammed and his mother had been so hospitable. We walked several miles to the nearest bus stop, where, next to it was an old shack café. It was unusual to see Northern European faces there, but before long, we were joined by a solitary Dutch boy of our age who was backpacking around North Africa. He said that he'd had a similar experience when he was down near a border town close to what was

4

previously Spanish Sahara. It had only recently changed hands to become Western Sahara the year before, and it had always been known as a hotbed of tribal wars. The aggrieved Moroccans contested Spain's colonial ownership of the place, so it was still very much an ever-continuing war zone.

Our Dutch friend told us that he was on a local bus when a number of tribesmen came on board. They talked among themselves for much of the journey until one of them drew a large curved dagger and held it to the Dutchman's throat. They instructed the driver to stop the bus, where they proceeded to throw him off headfirst into the desert. He was grateful that they didn't take his rucksack, which contained his passport and the little money that he possessed.

Prior to our conversation with him, it had never dawned on us that our own unfortunate experience was due entirely to the fact that Sue and the Australian girl were both wearing shorts! Our naivety was such that we never questioned the idea that Muslim people wouldn't be OK with that. After all, there were bikini-clad girls on some holiday resort beaches in Arab countries in other parts of the world, and every *Arabian Nights* style movie (1942) had scenes of beautiful semi-naked girls belly-dancing in Bedouin tents for the amusement of the menfolk.

Western audiences, particularly women, would find it highly romantic when the handsome Arab hero would say things like, "Bathe her in milk and scented oils and have her delivered to my tent!"

Although those Bedouin tent scenes appear mystical and exotic to the average Western movie-goer, the reality was that those young, nubile females were invariably previously captured infidel slaves. They were forced to dance and endure every carnal desire of their new Arab masters. Because Islam places such high value on the modesty and purity of their women by insisting they cover themselves with the burqa, niqab, or hijab, you would think that there would be no place in Islam for such a lewd display of immorality.

After all, no Muslim man would ever permit any woman of his to expose herself in such a way. Only infidel women could be treated to that level of utter contempt because of the impurity of their faith.

It is a widely accepted belief throughout the Islamic world that men have a God-given right to use non-believing females as sex slaves. This is repeated over and over again by some of the most prominent Islamic scholars of today. A recent example of it was made evident in England via a high-profile exposure, known as the "Rotherham case." Although various forms of belly-dancing had its origins in ancient India, over time it had travelled to Egypt, where it was then known as ghawazee. History informs us that Muslim warlords would set up schools in order to teach those slave-girls how to dance in as titillating a way as possible. Belly-dancing was also used as an important political tool. Having invited an opposing enemy leader to enter into talks over some form of peace agreement, what better way than to have your slave-girls dance for him and then provide him with whatever pleasures of the flesh he may desire. Today, belly-dancing is considered an art form, and is widely accepted in most modern countries as just a fun way to exercise.

Perhaps at this point I should explain the difference between the three forms of Islamic dress which is designed to protect the modesty of a Muslim woman. There is much confusion over the differences between the burqa, the niqab, and the hijab. The burqa is a full-body covering, including the face, in which the wearer can only see the world through a facial mesh covering. They appear mostly in black but in Afghanistan and Qatar they are often seen as pale blue. The niqab is again a full-body covering garment where only the eyes are revealed. The hijab ("to dress modestly") is what we see most of in the Western world where the woman wears a scarf covering her hair only.

We returned to the safety of our own creature comforts and to the familiarity of England's grey skies. But it was not long before the word "Islam" would appear again before us with news of the "Islamic uprising" in Iran; it was 1977. We watched as demonstrations raged and civil disobedience and resistance, against the then Shah of Persia, grew. Although principally driven by the Shia Muslim clergy, there were also many secular participants involved, in the form of left-wing activists and students, who were also aggrieved at the Westernisation and blatant capitalism now in their country. The Shah had brought Iran into the modern twentieth century, but there was discontent over his nepotism and his corruption.

The country had become decadent and extravagant under his reign. Tehran had a bustling café society, where the beautiful people would go to see and be seen. Men wore flared trousers and listened to Beatles music. Girls had bouffant hairdos and paraded themselves in mini-skirts. The hijab or niqab was rarely seen there except amongst some of the older women. Along with the rest of the Western world, Iran's wealthier youth was influenced by the latest fashions to come out of London's Carnaby St.

Iran's final "hour of discontent" had been orchestrated by a Shia clergyman by the name of Ayatollah Ruhollah Khomeini. He had been made prominent as early as 1963, when he accused the Shah of being "a wretched miserable man who has embarked upon the destruction of Islam in Iran." He deplored the Shah's relationship with the United States of America and his acceptance of the State of Israel. Khomeini was arrested and imprisoned, which caused mass riots. He was released eight months later and then in 1964 he was exiled. He believed that Western culture was a plague and an intoxication that must be eliminated. Only Shia Islam can be the true liberator from capitalism and that "martyrdom" and revolt play a vital part in the quest to purify the world for Islam. From his exile in Iraq and latterly from Neauphle-le-Chateau in northern France, he continued to pull the strings of subversion against the Shah's regime.

Khomeini developed the ideology of "guardianship by the jurists" and that government was best served by the rule of the imam scholars, thus ensuring that the holy scriptures and the law of Sharia (which is God's Law, not Man's Law) was preserved as the perfect template of life. The Qur'an, therefore, is not only the book of religious teaching: It also acts as the political constitution for the entire Islamic world. It has no borders nor boundaries. Muslims are obliged to obey the laws of the country of their residence only as long as they are in a minority and subservient in number to lack political control. The minute they find themselves in a position of superiority, then all Muslims must surrender themselves to the Law of Allah and the Sharia. They must strive to create that situation by any means possible, as no law can be higher than that of Allah's and no calling is greater than Islam.

After national chaos and the Black Friday Massacre, the Shah finally withdrew and fled his country on January 16th 1979. He was to be the last in the dynasty of the Shahs of Persia. The Ayatollah Khomeini was welcomed triumphantly by several million Iranians, eagerly awaiting the return of their religious salvation, "For there is no God but Allah, and Muhammed is his Messenger."

Understandably, not everyone was happy. Those that could foresee their future life in an enclosed totalitarian regime escaped the country to Great Britain and the U.S.A. Many others had neither the money nor the means to do so.

The first ruling of law made by the Ayatollah was the enforcement of women to wear the hijab or niqab in public places. Over one hundred thousand women marched in protest through the streets of Tehran. Islamist men attacked them and some of the women were stabbed to death. It wasn't too long before all objections were totally suppressed. Men who had previously been tolerant and full of soft, Western Judeo-Christian values quickly adopted their new role as a Muslim master of their own household, as per the holy decree. The Muslim man acknowledged the weakness of the Muslim woman both physically and intellectually, although they can share equal rights over such things as inheritance and property. The Qur'an acknowledges the differences between men and women and neither has more or less right to enter heaven.

The sheer speed at which the country of Iran was transformed, back into what many would consider to be something resembling the seventh century, was astonishing. The ordinary folk in the Western world looked on in total disbelief. They could see similarities between it and other totalitarian societies that had arisen earlier in the twentieth century, such as Communism and Nazism. This one appeared to have an additional sting in the tail in that it was a political ideology cloaked in a religion.

Soviet Communism was a godless, atheistic coup, where all devotion led to the all-consuming supremacy of the state. Nazism was based on the fulfilment of the Fuhrer's dream to restore the notion of purity of the Aryan race and to create his German Reich, all fuelled by Germany's humiliation at the Treaty of Versailles.

The Shia control of Iran and the subjugation of many personal liberties, including freedom of speech, faded from people's consciousness in the West, until, that is, a new word appeared in our English vocabulary, "fatwa" (meaning judgement).

Ayatollah Khomeini had issued a judgement of the death penalty against the Indian/English author Salman Rushdie for his book *Satanic Verses*. It was published by Viking Penguin Books in England in 1988, and won the Whitbread Award for novel of the year, for which Rushdie received £20,000 prize money. English book reviewers were oblivious of the significance of its mocking references to Islam and, before long, Muslims started to phone Viking Penguin Books with furious complaints that it was "blasphemous." In Bolton, Lancashire, a demonstration of around 7,000 Muslims burnt a copy of it in the town centre as a gesture of their revulsion.

In nearby Bradford there was a public burning of copies of Rushdie's book. Non-Muslims likened it to the Nazis burning the books of the Jews at the birth of the Second World War. The word spread, and Islamic countries around the world banned the sale of it. Frenzied displays of thousands of fanatical Muslims were seen on our television screens, screaming and shouting for Rushdie to be put to death. Substantial rewards were offered to the first Muslim to kill him.

Perhaps due to the unflappable English mentality, the average Brit couldn't get his head around what all the fuss was about. How could any rational thinking person get himself into such a lather? It was only a book of words to them. Right from their school playground chants, the English had always believed that "sticks and stones will break my bones, but words can never hurt me." The tectonic plate of the Islamic World and that of the infidel crusader were now starting to grind together once more. The faint rumblings of the rising of another caliphate of Islam could now be felt just below the surface. The last caliph had been silenced by Ataturk's Reforms in Turkey in 1924, which abolished the caliphate under the leadership of Abdulmecid II.

Chapter 2

MUHAMMED AND HIS MONOTHEIST MESSAGE

———∘◦◯◦∘———

M odern atheists, free thinkers, and men of science have continued to be wondrous at why any god with an infinite wisdom, a creator of all things from the amoeba to the blue whale, and all the galaxies, stars, and planets in the entire firmament of heaven, should wish to reveal himself... not to the great philosophers of Ancient Greece nor China, not to Sir Isaac Newton, Albert Einstein, or Professor Hawkins, but to an assortment of mostly illiterate, nomadic, desert-dwelling people from the Middle East. It seemed to defy all rationale.

And yet, from out of those lowly desert-dwelling beginnings, there are now 16 million Jews, 2.4 billion Christians and 1.8 billion Muslims living in the world today. Collectively, they have contributed more to man's knowledge and advancement, while at the same time causing more death, misery, destruction, and failure than any other section of humanity. Perhaps we should look closer at those desert-dwelling beginnings.

The Arabian Peninsula is as inhospitable a place as you will find anywhere on earth. The shifting sands offer little in the way of vegetative sustenance, and only the hardiest breeds of Jacob sheep, goats, and camels can offer a meagre living for the nomadic tribes who call it home. Survival is the name of the game, and, as with all nomadic peoples, they never stay long enough in any one place to create a lasting legacy for civilisation.

With a constant battle for survival comes an intense loyalty to one's own tribe, and myths, legends, and campfire story-telling play a big part in the foundation of their religious beliefs. Rare and exotic stones found in the desert, or traded, could be said to hold mystical powers, and most of the pagan tribes there had their own assortment of them. They were revered, and in several small towns were housed in what was called a Ka'aba, a box-shaped building. They proved to be a handy source of revenue as pilgrims would travel far and wide to come and pay their homage. The town of Mecca had a very special one in the form of a black stone, believed to have fallen from the sky. It is known as al-Hajar al-Aswad. The natural conclusion would be to say that it is a meteorite, but no scientific evidence is available as it has remained far too holy an object to facilitate any kind of inspection.

Nobody knows exactly when it first arrived there, but it was believed to have been sent at the time of Adam and Eve. It arrived on earth as brilliant white, but over time it has blackened with the acceptance of the sins of men. Muslims believe that Abraham and his son Ishmael built the Ka'aba at Mecca, and having found the black stone, placed it as its Eastern cornerstone, which is where it remains to this day. I point out that it is not the stone nor the Ka'aba itself that is being worshipped when we see hundreds of thousands of Muslims uniformly walking round the Ka'aba seven times. Muslims are not permitted to worship any graven image or object, only Allah. It is the focal point of veneration only by its direct association with both Abraham and their founder, the Prophet Muhammed, who is believed to have kissed the stone.

However, after Abraham, the building did not remain as a shrine to a monotheist god. Pre-Islam, the Ka'aba contained as many as 360 objects of worship, which amplified its religious value amongst the pagan tribes and the visiting pilgrims.

As I explained at the beginning of this book, mine is not to bludgeon one set of scriptures in the Old and New Testaments against another set of scriptures in the Qur'an. I have to leave that to the academics and the religious scholars on both sides, who have been squabbling over it for the past fourteen hundred years, and are unlikely to stop anytime soon.

I'm more interested in offering the layperson, the non-believer, a basic insight into the foundation of the problem of conflict, where it is now, and what we can do about it, if we plan on getting along in the future.

The principal problem lies in the fact that the entire Judeo-Arab world claims to be descendant from Abraham. Abraham's wife, Sarah (Sar'ai), was believed to be infertile, and having reached the ripe old age of 75 she still hadn't provided him with a child. In order to fulfil the Abrahamic Covenant found in Genesis 15, it was Sarah's idea that Abraham could take their young Egyptian servant-girl, Hagar, to have a child with. She was to give birth to a healthy boy; Abraham was 86 at this time. During Hagar's pregnancy, Sarah became jealous of her, and so Hagar fled the household, during which time she received a message from God via an angel, telling her that she was to call the child Ishmael (Ismail), and that "He shall be a warrior, living in conflict with his kinsmen." Hagar then returned to Abraham's house to continue serving her mistress.

As part of the covenant with God, and at the age of 13, Ishmael was included in a mass circumcision of all of the men in the Abraham household, including the 99-year-old Abraham.

During the covenant, Abraham was told that Sarah was also to have a boy-child; She was 90 years old by this time. Abraham was also told that they were to call the boy Isaac (Ishaq), and that his covenant would be established through Isaac and not his elder half-brother, Ishmael. Here lies the keystone to the Jews believing that they alone are the chosen ones of God, because their Jewish lineage lies there with Isaac. When Abraham was instructed to kill his son as a sacrifice, the Bible refers to "his only son, Isaac." Christians also err on the side of the Jews with that one. The Qur'an has no mention of which son it was, and Muslims, understandably, stake their claim, insisting that it was Ishmael who was chosen for the sacrifice by his father, not Isaac, and that the Jews have twisted the truth.

After Abraham was relieved of that task and rewarded with a sheep to slaughter instead, Abraham was to enquire of God what was to befall Ishmael.

He was answered by God telling him that Ishmael would be blessed, fruitful, and will multiply him exceedingly. "Twelve

princes shall he begat, and I shall make him a great nation."
(Genesis 17).

Once Sarah had given birth to Isaac, she wanted rid of Hagar
and Ishmael altogether, saying to Abraham, "Get rid of that
slave woman and her son, for that slave woman's son will
never share in the inheritance with my son, Isaac." Naturally,
Abraham was reluctant to do so, until God spoke to him
again, telling him that "in Isaac your seed shall be called,"
but Abraham knew that Ishmael would survive no matter
what happened, because God had also revealed that he
would "make a nation of the son of the bondwoman."
Abraham led Hagar and her young son out into the desert.
He gave them bread and water and abandoned them there.

Ishmael did indeed go on to begat 12 princes: Nebaioth,
Kedar, Adbeel, Mibsam, Mishma, Dumah, Massa, Hadad,
Tema, Jetur, Naphish, and Kedemah. They became fathers of
the Arab nations as we know it today.

Now you see the reason for the great dividing canyon
between the descendants of Isaac (the Jews) and the
descendants of Ishmael (the Arabs). It is irredeemably
gouged in the aggregate of their history.

Before the discovery of oil, the whole region was of little
interest to any conquering army. Mostly, people were just
passing through it.

By seventh-century standards, the town of Mecca could have
been described as "multicultural." In addition to Jews,
Christians, local pagan tribes, and passing tradespeople of
many obscure faiths, it was known as a place of religious
tolerance, diversity, and open discussion.

The leading local tribe in Mecca was the Quraysh, of which a young and charismatic man called Muhammed was one; He was born in 570 AD. If there was ever such a thing as a social services department in sixth-century Mecca, then Muhammed would have been deserving of its help. In his infancy, his mother was widowed, and when he was six years of age she died.

One can only imagine that being brought up by a single mother in that time and place would undoubtedly mean that the family would be on the periphery of society, poor, and well down the pecking order, socially. His uncle, Abu Talib, who was a man of some standing in the community, eventually took him in. Muhammed was put to work as a camel herder and traveller, and we are informed by the Sunni scholars that he never received an education and was unable to read or write.

Nonetheless, Muhammed soon became known for his sound judgement and wisdom. After a flash flood, an event for which Mecca was well renowned, the Ka'aba suffered serious damage and had to be rebuilt. The precious black stone was to be reinstalled, and there was much arguing amongst four of the clan leaders as to which one of them should have the honour and the worthiness to place it back into its position in the east corner of the building. They decided that the next person to enter the room would be the arbiter of the decision.

It just happened to be Muhammed. He placed a carpet on the floor and instructed each chief to take hold of a corner of the carpet. Muhammed then placed the black stone in the centre of the carpet and they carefully lifted it into position, thus giving equal status and honour to all four of them without preference.

At the age of 25, fortune, and perhaps a little opportunism, favoured him, and he met and married a rich 40-year-old widow called Khadijah. It is believed that Muhammed proved to be a persuasive and successful salesman in Khadijah's trading business and that together they enjoyed a lifestyle that we would probably refer to as middle class. Muhammed's poverty days were now well behind him.

It would appear that their marriage was a happy one, and Khadijah was well known for her kindliness and her caring nature. They were also reported as being monogamous during their years together. As time progressed, Muhammed became more contemplative and spiritual, going off alone for days at a time. In particular, he would spend time in a cave at Mount Hira, not far from Mecca; he was 40 years of age by this time. During one such trip he received a visit from the angel Gabriel, who informed him that he was to be God's final chosen messenger. The last Holy Prophet.

Early reports suggest that his visions were accompanied by mysterious seizures, and that Muhammed became deeply distressed. But with the passage of time and endless debate between scholars of both Sunni and Shia, that idea seems to have faded. Upon returning home he was greatly comforted by his wife and his immediate family. Khadijah became his first convert and "The Mother of the Believers."

Muhammed's message from his revelation was that of monotheism. There is but only one God, Allah. Therefore,

Islam rejects the Christian belief in the Holy Trinity of God the Father, God the Son, and God the Holy Ghost. Also, Jesus was not the Son of God but merely a prophet. All previous prophets were unsatisfactory in the eyes of Allah in bringing the message of salvation to mankind. Allah has therefore chosen Muhammed to be his last messenger and to be the final Holy Prophet. He was to warn mankind of its eschatological punishment (the final judgement), and they must not continue to worship false deities or idols, the like of which were contained within the Ka'aba.

In 613 AD, three years after his first revelation, Muhammed began to preach his message on the streets of Mecca. This was mostly ignored by the general public, and in many cases people mocked him in exactly the same way that people would mock someone today if they were to declare that they were the final messenger of God.

As I said previously, Mecca was a tolerant and multicultural place at that time. But, there is only so much tolerance people will adhere to when it comes to affecting their pockets. The Ka'aba was the major producer of the town's income. Innkeepers and merchants of all kinds made their living from the pilgrims that flocked there. Muhammed was also beginning to attract converts to his new monotheist beliefs, which was not going down too well with the town's clan leaders and, in particular, his own Quraysh family elders. He was becoming a seriously disruptive nuisance as far as they were concerned.

One can connect the similarity with Jesus, when he also stepped that bit too far by upsetting the stalls of the money

19

lenders and pigeon sellers in the Temple. Caiaphas and his cronies controlled the Temple and, obviously, the rents from the stall holders. Jesus was also gathering converts and, similarly, was becoming a seriously disruptive nuisance. Caiaphas had to think of a way to get rid of him.

Rich merchants did everything they could to convince Muhammed to give up his preaching, and they offered him numerous incentives to do so. But Muhammed refused point-blank to deny his calling from Allah. It was at that point that things started to turn very nasty indeed, and Muslims say that a persecution of Muhammed's followers began.

Other scholars disagree and lay blame on Muhammed.

Sumayyah bint Khayyat was a slave-girl to a man called Abu Jahl, and when she refused to deny Muhammed as the holy messenger of Allah, Abu Jahl thrust a spear into her. She became the first martyr to Islam.

In the year 619 AD, both Muhammed's beloved wife, Khadijah, and his uncle, Abu Talib, died. It was known as the "Year of Sorrow." This proved to be a serious threat to Muhammed and his followers because they had always enjoyed the protection of Abu Talib, but now they were very vulnerable.

The following year, Muhammed was to experience a mysterious night-long journey, known as the Isra and Mi'raj, which took him from Mecca to Jerusalem. It is said that he was lifted up on a winged horse and carried to the furthest mosque, which was at Jerusalem. He travelled with the angel Gabriel and there he toured both heaven and hell.

Whilst there, he also met Abraham, Moses, Jesus and others, and after meeting Abraham, Muhammed went up alone to meet with God himself, Allah the Most High. Allah instructed Muhammed that his followers must pray to him 50 times a day, but on his way back down to earth, Muhammed encountered Moses again, who told him to go back up to Allah because 50 is just too high a figure. Muhammed then went back and forth three times until Allah finally agreed that five times a day was sufficient. Anyone who did that would be rewarded tenfold.

Following the death of Muhammed's uncle, Abu Talib, Abu Lahab had taken over as the leader of the Banu Hashim tribe of the Quraysh and he immediately withdrew all clan protection for Muhammed and his followers.

This would mean that in the event of his murder, nobody would avenge his death. This was an important part of the social order of things, because tit-for-tat, an eye for an eye, and a tooth for a tooth, was what kept the balance of power amongst the clans. Everyone behaved themselves because they knew that if you killed another man's son then he would be honour-bound to come and kill yours or worse.

Chapter 3

HIJRAH: MUHAMMED FLEES TO MEDINA

Muhammed learned of a plot to kill him, and he had no alternative but to slip away out of Mecca along with his followers. The town of Medina was approximately 280 miles north of Mecca, and in June of 622 AD, Muhammed and his followers fled there on what is known as the Hijrah, or migration, and they became known as Muhajirun, or emigrants. The Islamic calendar was to begin from this date and not the date of Muhammed's birth.

Medina was an agricultural oasis town. It had endured nearly a hundred years of slaughter and counter-slaughter over even the most trivial of land disputes, mainly between the resident Arabs and the Jews. Upon hearing of Muhammed's arrival, a delegation decided that he would make the perfect arbiter in such circumstances, for he was known for his Solomon-like ability. The elders decided that they and their entire fellow citizens would subject themselves to the rule of his judgement. Muhammed's first task was to implement a "Constitution of Medina," granting rights and duties to the various tribes, and that included the "people of the book," who were the Jews and the Christians. At first, he wanted to appease them in some ways; the Qur'an included much from the Bible, although some of it was not transcribed with total accuracy.

Once some of the Medinan leaders became Muslim converts, Muhammed's seat of power became more established. Jews in particular could never accept Muhammed as their prophet, because he was not of the line of David, which would contradict their own prophetic scriptures. At first, he said that Jews and Christians could attain their salvation in heaven through their own beliefs, but he was later to revoke that idea.

So far, after 13 years, Muhammed had only managed to convince a hundred to a hundred and fifty people of his status as the one true Holy Prophet, and the last messenger of Allah. He sent out word to the few remaining followers in Mecca to come and move to Medina. His power base was growing rapidly, by the day. The Constitution of Medina became the beginnings of the Islamic concept of the union of state and religion combined. Things were about to show a major change. Muhammed was to undergo a metamorphosis into a "Warrior Prophet."

The Qur'an, whose first part shows tolerance and kindly wisdom, known as the Meccan part, was about to display a level of savage brutality in the second part, the Medinan, the likes of which cannot be found in any other religion that still exists today.

Muhammed continued to receive revelations from Allah, and the most recent one told him to avenge and attack the Meccans. The Quranic directives now seemed to be based more on matters of state and war, as opposed to its previous biblical instructions leading to one's heavenly salvation, as with Christian doctrines of the New Testament. It also leant heavily on the fact that Allah commands his followers to obey at all times the orders of his holy messenger, the Prophet Muhammed. This is repeated many times over, just in case it didn't sink in the first time.

In March of 624 AD, Muhammed, along with three hundred of his Muslim warriors, set out to attack Meccan caravans. As they lay in ambush, word got back to Mecca and so the elders sent forth a force to confront them. It was to be known as the Battle of Badr. Although outnumbered three-to-one, Muhammed's army enjoyed a resounding victory. To his Muslim followers this merely confirmed the prophet's divine relationship with Allah. (An example of such a belief would be repeated some thirteen hundred years later in Afghanistan with the defeat of the Russians.)

Muhammed explained that victory would not have been achieved at Badr without the assistance of a host of invisible angels at their side.

The victory at the Battle of Badr did not bode well for the three Jewish tribes back home in Medina. They were the Banu Qaynuqa, the Banu Quyrayza, and the Banu Nadir. In the early days, they had all been compliant in accepting Muhammed as their arbiter, their Lord Chief Justice, so-to-speak. They had not anticipated his meteoric rise to absolute power.

Pagans and Arab tribes were converting to Islam in their droves, mostly with a convert-or-else clause attached! The Jews had already made it clear that their scriptures could not allow them to accept Muhammed as their final prophet. Following another revelation from Allah, Muhammed accused the Jews of deliberately corrupting their own scriptures in order to eliminate the evidence that he was the prophet and the messenger of Allah. No evidence of such a corruption has ever been found by scholars from any of the three great religions. Early verses of tolerance contained within the Meccan part of the Qur'an were beginning to be abrogated by later verses.

Muhammed could not allow his divine calling to be in question.

Bukhari 53:392 explains it more clearly when Muhammed said to the Jews:

> If you embrace Islam, you will be safe. You should know that the earth belongs to Allah and his Apostle, and I want to expel you from this land. So, if anyone amongst you owns property, he is permitted to sell it, otherwise, you should know that the earth belongs to Allah and his Apostle.

Forced conversion by intimidation became a precedent for Islamists to follow to this very day.

First to go was the Jewish tribe of the Banu Qaynuqa. After a killing and counter-killing, the Muslims then felt justified in expelling them into exile and confiscating their property and lands. It was to be included in the Qur'an that 20% of all spoils would be paid to Muhammed, the rest divided between his followers. Muslims began to get a taste for war and plunder. His armies grew at an alarming speed, and converting to Islam could prove highly profitable for a young Muslim man. Not only could he gain money and riches, but also wives and sex slaves aplenty, and all with the blessing of his newly acquired religion. Some expressed an uneasiness at raping the women, and what would become of the possible outcome of children? They were assured that Allah was the creator of all life, and therefore, all such children would be born into the warm embrace of Islam: Hey Presto! Licence granted. Again, if you go to YouTube, you will see some of the most prominent imams of today preaching this verbatim that the taking of infidel sex slaves is an acceptable practice.

The Banu Nadir Jews were to endure a similar fate after Muhammed believed that they were plotting to kill him. He laid siege to their community and expelled them from their lands. Again the spoils were taken, but it is written that this time the property was exclusively reserved for the prophet. (One must ask oneself how his followers felt about that.)

Most well known of all, even to the most unenlightened of non-believers, was the story of what eventually happened to the third Jewish community, the Banu Qurayza.

The Meccans were anxious to regain their prestige after such a humiliating defeat by the Muslims at the Battle of Badr. It was logical that the two Jewish tribes which had been exiled by Muhammed would also be keen to seek revenge and form an alliance with the Meccans.

Muhammed got wind of the possibility of an attack and began to prepare. He was now proving to be a brilliant military strategist, to add to his already remarkable list of achievements. The Meccans gathered together a substantial force of some 4,000 foot soldiers, 300 horse cavalry, and 1,000 men on camels.

Again, Muhammed was informed in advance. He then knew that it would take around a week for them to arrive at Medina. He decided that he would take defensive action, and every able-bodied person joined in the building of enormous trenches to defy the horse cavalry and the camels. Only the Banu Qurayza Jews were exempt, but they did provide the tools. They had reached an agreement with Muhammed and were understandably in fear. They thought it most prudent to remain neutral. The leader of the Banu Nadir Jews tried to persuade them that it would be in their best interests to turn against the Muslims, and when they saw the size of the Meccan army, they agreed. What followed was to be known as the "Battle of the Trench." Yet again, Muhammed was one step ahead of them and he learned of their betrayal. He did not want his own men to learn of it, lest it cause them to become demoralised. The Meccans tried several times to breach Muhammed's trench system, but failed. It was unusual in that the warfare they were used to was always on open plains, clear and brutal. The capture of Medina seemed impossible. After weeks, everyone was running out of food and water. Camels and horses were dying and the weather was blazing hot in the day and freezing at night. The Meccans packed up and left.

The Meccan retreat was the ultimate humiliation. They had come to destroy the Muslims and failed miserably. It was to have a serious effect on its trade after that.

Muhammed now turned his attention to the Jews, in revenge for their perceived betrayal. For the next 25 days he besieged the Banu Qurayza with an unprecedented brutality. The women and children were divided up as sex slaves and child slaves respectively, and their possessions and land was divided amongst all the Muslims. Reports vary, but as many as 900 Jewish men were tied and bound. Muhammed had trenches dug in the old marketplace in Medina, which still functions as the market today. The men were led out in batches and Muhammed proceeded to chop their heads off until all were finished with.

Only one woman was included in that mass execution. She had been talking to Aisha, Muhammed's favourite wife (and I shall refer to her later), when her name was called out. Aisha is reported as saying, "I shall never forget her cheerfulness and great laughter when she knew that she was to be killed."

Muhammed justified his actions in two ways. Firstly, to show mercy would be to show weakness. Secondly, he was able to refer to the Jews' own Bible, the Torah, Deuteronomy 20:10-14:

When you march up to attack a city, make its people an offer of peace. If they accept and open their gates, all the people in it shall be subject to forced labour and shall work for you. If they refuse to make peace and engage you in battle, lay siege to that city. When the Lord your God delivers it into your hand, put to the sword all men who are in it. As for the women, the children, the livestock, and everything else in the city, you may take these as plunder for yourselves. And you may use the plunder the Lord your God gives you from your enemies.

It is presently almost beyond our comprehension for an act of such outright barbarism to happen in today's globalised world, where news is instant. Assyrian and Coptic Christians may beg to differ. Their crucifixions and beheadings are happening as a daily occurrence, as I write. Shamefully, such atrocities hardly get a couple of lines of copy from the Western news media agencies.

Mecca had lost its trading partners in Syria and both the morale and the economy were in decline. Leaders in the town were in serious discussions as to whether converting to Islam may be the only inevitable option left open to them.

The followers of the Holy Prophet had always previously prayed to the city of Jerusalem, but in a request to Allah, Muhammed had asked to change the direction of prayer to Mecca and to the Ka'aba of Abraham. Allah granted such permission, and, in accordance with tradition, it was to remain the place of pilgrimage. Although Jerusalem was of huge importance, being the place of Mohammed's ascension to heaven, it was also the holiest city for the Jews and the Christians, and Islam needed its own place of supreme worship. Mecca was not only the place of Abraham and Ishmael: It was also the birthplace of Muhammed. Mecca, Medina, then Jerusalem remains the order of superiority to the Islamic world.

Quranic verse states that Muslims must attend the annual pilgrimage to the Ka'aba, known as the Hajj, meaning "to intend a journey." With Muhammed's preoccupation in defending Medina his followers had not done so.

Muhammed therefore ordered them to prepare for the journey; the year was 628 AD.

Upon hearing that as many as 1,400 Muslims were heading their way for the pilgrimage, Umrah (meaning secondary or lesser pilgrimage), naturally the Meccans were more than a little concerned, and sent out a deployment of some 200 cavalry. Muhammed managed to avoid them by taking a different route. The faithful arrived at a place called al-Hudaybiyya, not far from the city. Emissaries were sent out immediately to negotiate a peace settlement with Muhammed. He wanted to show the Meccans that when it came to "pilgrimage," Islam is a religion of peace. (Where have you heard that before?)

A ten-year treaty was signed as follows.

"In your name, Oh God.

This is the treaty of peace between Muhammed Ibn Abdullah and Suhayl Ibn Amr. They have agreed to allow their arms to rest for ten years. During this time, each party shall be secure, and neither shall injure the other; no secret damage shall be inflicted, but honesty and honour shall prevail between them. Whoever in Arabia wishes to enter into a treaty or covenant with Muhammed, can do so, and whoever wishes to enter into a treaty or covenant with the Quraysh, can do so. And if a Qurayshite comes without the permission of his guardian to Muhammad, he shall be delivered up to the Quraysh; but if, on the other hand, one of Muhammed's people comes to the Quraysh, he shall not be delivered up to Muhammed. This year, Muhammed, with his companions, must withdraw from Mecca, but next year, he may come to Mecca and remain for three days, yet without weapons except those of a traveller; The swords remaining in their sheaths."

(The Statement of the Treaty of Hudaybiyyah)

Many of Muhammed's followers were not happy with the treaty, having travelled all that way with their sacrificial animals for pilgrimage, only to be turned away and told to come back next year. They grossly underestimated Muhammed's canny wisdom as a military strategist. He was very aware that the Meccans were well prepared to repel his attack, should he make it at this time.

Muhammed had no intention of keeping the treaty. Instead, he would go away and massively consolidate his military capability, in order to ensure total victory against the Meccans at some time in the future, and when they would least expect it.

In the meantime, there was still a question of the Jews to deal with. Khaybar was an oasis town about 90 miles from Medina. There, his old former fellow citizens, the Banu Nadir Jews, were still feeling a grudge at being forcibly removed from Medina minus everything they owned in life. They were constantly causing trouble in trying to unite the other Jewish tribes to engage with them. The Battle of Khaybar was over fairly quickly and the Jews surrendered. Despite previously losing everything, the Banu Nadir had quickly replenished their fortunes at Khaybar in both farming and business. One can delineate a clear difference in the mindset of the Jew, whose prime interest always errs on the side of enterprise and commerce, and the more nomadic Arab's propensity toward tribal warfare, rape, and plunder.

It is not difficult to imagine the absolute terror the Banu Nadir were experiencing at that time, knowing full well what had happened to their fellow brethren, the Banu Qurayza Jews. This time, Muhammed came up with a new idea.

He was to impose what was called jizya. The Jews could continue with their enterprises in peace, as long as they paid the jizya tax of 50% to the Muslims. Although their possessions, women, and land was confiscated for a second time, they could continue to live on, work, and cultivate it. They would become the Dhimmi, (meaning second-class citizen or an inferior low-life person.) Although this term originally applied only to Jews, it later became applicable to all non-Muslims living in a Muslim controlled area, which is known as a caliphate. The jizya and the status of Dhimmi would be instated into Islamic law.

The jizya has been regularly applied in varying forms throughout the Islamic world from that day forward. Never think for a second that it could play no part in our modern world. Once it is written in the holy scriptures, it is commanded by Allah and His Messenger, and therefore it cannot be revoked or questioned. Muslims pay a tax of their own called zakat.

In return for the payment of jizya, the Dhimmi would be guaranteed protection from any possible marauding aggression. Muhammed had to ensure that every Muslim was fully conversant in the art of war... and every Dhimmi was not!

The people of nearby Fadak, who'd assisted the Jews at Khaybar, made a plea for leniency in exchange for surrender. It comes as no surprise that they also suffered the consequences of then having the status of Dhimmi.

Muhammed sent letters to several leaders throughout the Arab world, extending all the way from Persia to the Yemen, advising them that it would be in their best interests to convert to Islam, and that included Heraclius, the Emperor of the Eastern Roman Empire, known as the Byzantine Empire. Muhammed's tactic obviously reveals that he placed enormous value on the advantage of psychological warfare. Your enemy is already considerably weakened when, in advance, he is allowed time to perceive the absolute horror and brutality of the outcome if he resists. Victory by terror! It is a tactic Muslims have successfully continued to employ up to this very day and which, following 9/11, prompted President George W. Bush to make his "War on Terror!" speech, only to follow it up by saying, "Islam is a religion of peace."

Two years after signing the ten-year Treaty of Hudaybiyyah, Muhammed marched a force of 10,000 of his warrior converts on Mecca. He justified it by saying that the Banu Bakr, who had links to Mecca, had raided against the Banu Khuza'a, who had links to Muhammed. That was enough to nullify the treaty.

Most of the Meccans had already resigned themselves to the inevitability that to convert and surrender to Islam was the easiest option in staying alive. They had yielded themselves to that humiliating notion of appeasement. The Muslims had total conviction in their belief of success, whereas most of the Meccans were resigned to fear and indifference. It is a serious lesson to be learned by our own modern-day politicians in the Western world, when dealing with today's spread of the Islamists. Appeasement is never an option against a totalitarian mindset. 2% Conviction can destroy 98% of Indifference at the blink of an eye.

Chapter 4

ISLAM'S SUCCESS, AND THE DEATH OF MUHAMMED

———∘⊙⊙∘———

There were few casualties in the taking of Mecca. Muhammed was now master of all he surveyed. It must have been most gratifying to finally claim mastery over the Quraysh, his own people, who had mocked his self-proclaimed prophetic relationship with Allah and had rejected him. From the humble orphan boy in their midst, he had outsmarted, outflanked, and outmanoeuvred them at every turn.

His first job, after ensuring their total submission to Islam (the meaning of the word Islam is "submission" or enslavement to Allah), was to destroy all 360 deities and pagan idols contained within the Ka'aba. Only the holy black cornerstone of Abraham remained sacred. It is written that he did spare some images of Jesus and Mary. Muhammed compared Mary, the mother of Christ, to his own deceased wife, Khadijah.

Muhammed's belief in the infallibility of his cause was now unstoppable. Every successful military campaign (and I haven't mentioned all of them in his life's meteoric journey) brought with it untold wealth from the spoils of war, and both the liberty and licence for his followers to exploit every avenue of lust and savage brutality known to man.

Within two weeks of taking Mecca, Muhammed was ready to move on again. Now, along with his own 10,000 troops, he had conscripted another 2,000 Meccans who had all "embraced Islam." It would appear that his thirst for war and conquest was now unquenchable, or was it just his absolute determination to force heavenly salvation on mankind, dependent on which way you look at it?

Throughout many of the campaigns, Muhammed would receive revelations and directives from Allah, which would then be verbally communicated to his men.

Next in line were the Bedouins of Hawazin and Thaqif of Ta'if. They had long been enemies of the Meccans, and now they would be of the opinion that Muhammed, who was a Meccan Quraysh, would also be their enemy. The Hawazin and the Thaqif had resigned themselves to the inevitability of war with Muhammed and had mobilised their troops accordingly. To see such a vast movement of militia was rare in those days, and Muhammed's men were overconfident that their sheer volume of 12,000 would be sufficient to win the day. They were to engage at the Battle of Hunayn.

The Hawazin and Thaqif lay in ambush, and when the Muslims made camp, their enemies showered down on them with arrows. The Muslims got up and ran, leaving only a few to stand and fight. Muhammed cried out, "Come on, people, I am the messenger of Allah, son of Abdullah." Then he called out to Allah, "Oh, Allah, send down your help!" His men returned and defeated the enemy. But Muhammed rebuked them for their cowardice.

The Qur'an 9:25 recalls:

> Assuredly, Allah did help you in many battlefields and on the day of Hunayn: Behold! Your great numbers elated you, but they availed you naught. The land, for all that it is wide, did constrain you, and ye turned back in retreat.
>
> But Allah did pour his calm on the messenger and on the believers, and sent down forces which ye saw not. He punished the unbelievers: Thus doth he reward those without Faith.

This time, so vast were the spoils that Muhammed didn't know what to do with much of it. There was a total of 24,000 camels and 6,000 prisoners of war, to start with. These people were mainly the nomadic Bedouin. They had brought their women, children, and livestock along to be near to the battle site. Muhhamed's Believers were greatly rewarded with camels, women and child sex slaves that day, and one can only imagine the orgy of indulgence that ensued from that.

The call of "Allahu Akbar!", which means "God is greater," was first called out by Muhammed on the battlefield of Badr. It was interpreted as meaning that "God is greater than our enemies." It is also used in general conversation as an awareness of God's presence, and as a reminder to the believer that he is always a slave to the service of Allah and to no other. Islamists throughout the centuries have chanted it in order to instil fear into hearts of the non-believers. It remains to this day a useful tool in the armoury of their oldest game of psychological warfare. However, to the modern-day infidel crusader, or right-wing activist, it merely acts as a red rag to a bull.

Every Muslim must declare the shahadah, which is the creed of the religion, in a similar way that the Roman Catholics have their Catechism. The shahadah is as follows: "I testify that there is no God but Allah, and I testify that Muhammed is the messenger of Allah." It is the very first words a Muslim must whisper into the ears of his newborn child, and the very last words heard on the lips of a dying man.

On June 8th 632 AD, Muhammed died at Medina in the arms of his favourite wife, Aisha, shortly after making his final Hajj pilgrimage to the Ka'aba in Mecca that had marked ten years following on from his original migration to Medina. In those ten years he had laid a foundation stone that would change the world.

His final Hajj was also to set the precedent for all Muslims throughout the entire world to attempt to make their own pilgrimage to the holy site at least once in their life, if not every year. They pray each day towards it and in death they are buried towards it.

It is a 1,400-year-old murder mystery story as to how Muhammed really died, but most likely, it was at the hands of his Jewish slave girl who poisoned him with contaminated meat. However, not all Jews were exempt from Muhammed's affections. Safiyyah, for example, was a stunningly beautiful seventeen year old Jewish girl who had just witnessed Muhammed decapitate her father, her uncle, her brothers and cousins. Her mother and sisters were given to his followers as wives and sex slaves. Her husband,

Kinana, was the town treasurer at Khaybar when her fellow Jews were offered the status of Dhimmi. Muhammed was convinced that Kinana was not divulging the whereabouts of some of the treasures which were rightly Muhammed's spoils of victory, and so he decided that Kinana needed a little persuading. He lit a bonfire of sticks on Kinana's chest. At the same time an informant told Muhammed that Kinana had been spotted going each morning to the site of an old ruin outside of the town. Muhammed sent his men to excavate it and the treasure was found. Muhammed proceeded to chop his head off and then he immediately seduced Kinana's seventeen year old widow. He declared her to be his new wife, and so it was not rape. Nonconsensual sex does not seem to appear in Islam. The word 'Rape' does not exist in the Qur'an, there is no such thing.

Of all of the wives Muhammed collected along the way, there is no doubt that Aisha was his favourite. The list of his wives is as follows:

Khadijah, Sawda, Aisha, Hafsa, Zaynab, Hind, Zaynab (Bint Jahsh), Juwayriyya, Ramla, Rayhana, Safiyyah, Maymunah, and Maria.

Aisha was the daughter of Abu Bakr, who was one of Muhammed's most loyal and trusted friends. Next to Khadijah, Abu Bakr was the first to accept Muhammed as the Holy Prophet and the messenger of Allah. He was wealthy and influential. Following the death of Khadijah in 619 AD, it is believed that Abu Bakr offered Muhammed his six-year-old daughter to be his wife. There is no doubt that

Muhammed was infatuated with the child. She was highly intelligent, inquisitive, lively, and amusing. Muhammed accepted her and at the first sign of puberty, when she was nine years old, he consummated the marriage; he was 53 years old by this time. Aisha became a driving force in the embryonic days of Islam. She was astute and greatly admired, and even went into battle. After his death, she continued to live for 44 years and is responsible for contributing some 2,210 Hadiths (meaning "reports" or "accounts").

By the time of his death, Muhammed had taken control of the entire Arabian Peninsula. He had removed all traces of the people's varied polytheistic beliefs, going back thousands of years, and replaced it with his own version of a monotheism that has control over every single facet of the believer's life: from what he eats, what time he gets up, to what time he goes to bed, to how he conducts his business, who he befriends, and who he is commanded to hate. It controls his sex life and his children's life, from birth to the grave. It is his religion, his government, his judge, and his jury, for all is as one under Allah.

The Christian world separates the church from the state and "renders unto Caesar that which is Caesar's and unto God that which is God's."

Islam has no such definition. No government in any Islamic-controlled country could ever introduce a form of legislation which is in any way conflicting with the teachings of the Holy Qur'an. Consider, for example, our government's recent introduction of equal gay rights, which is in defiance of the Bible's teachings in Leviticus 18:22, "For men shall not lie together as with a woman, for it is an abomination to the Lord." Islam has no such yielding. The true Islamists demand death for homosexuals by "throwing them from the mountaintops" or a high-rise building will do if there is no mountain close at hand. Islam has spent the last 1,400 years with its scholars, muftis, and imams in perpetual conflict over the interpretations of the scriptures, many of which were written as late as the ninth century AD.

The Qur'an contains all the verbal revelations by God to Muhammed via the angel Gabriel, the first of which happened in December of 609 AD and the last being in the year of his death in 632 AD.

The Qur'an is the central religious text of Islam.

The Sunnah is the record of verbally transmitted sayings, deeds, and actions of the Holy Prophet Muhammed. It is defined as the path, the way, and the manner in which the prophet lived his life, his practices, and his traditions which are deemed to be the exemplar for all Muslims to follow. For it is written that Muhammed was the perfect man!

The Qur'an and the Hadith of Gabriel command six articles of faith within Islam:

(1) Belief in Allah, for there is only one God.

(2) Belief in the Angels.

(3) Belief in the Holy Books of the Taurat (Torah), the Gospel, and the Qur'an.

(4) Belief in the Prophets.

(5) Belief in the Day of Judgement.

(6) Belief in God's predestination.

There must be nothing dearer to the true believer than his faith.

Having said that, and for the purpose of this book, I'm insufficiently equipped to dissect and offer credible argument in the discussion of the holy scriptures. I could never claim to be an Islamic theologian.

All I offer is a chronology of historical events leading up to today's disagreement with the ideology of Islam and its effect on the rest of the world: Where did it all go wrong? And what can we do about it?

There are those who will argue, with some justification, that this book lacks balance and has little reference to the early Quranic Meccan verses, which are partly taken from the Torah. Within it, there are examples of tolerance, kindness, benevolence, wisdom, and understanding. The problem lies in that much of that is abrogated by the later intolerant and violent verses in the Medinan verses – in particular, the numerous references to the destruction of the Jews and the Christians, which are referred to as the infidels or the kafir and, even within the faith itself, the brutal finality of the death sentence for apostasy. Like the Mafia, once you are a Muslim it appears that you can never leave it for an alternative faith.

Following the death of Muhammed, there was no clear heir apparent. Therein lies the birth of a division within Islam which continues to be responsible for the shedding of copious amounts of blood from that day to this. As long as a Sunni Muslim and a Shia Muslim exist, there will never be peace between them. However, one thing will always unite them, and that is their divine guided mission to convert, subjugate, or kill the unbeliever infidel, the kafir.

Modern-day moderate Muslims, who live amongst us, carry the burden of that fact with a certain amount of embarrassment, which usually ends up with an open denial. They regularly blame "misinterpretation" as being at fault. The fact is that the vitriol is there and available in the first place, to be accepted or rejected by today's believers. Moderates usually retaliate by saying that there is evidence of a dreadful doctrine within the Jewish and Christian faiths also. True! But nobody in today's modern world is going to tolerate a section of the Roman Catholic community who suddenly decides to reintroduce the Spanish Inquisition, or for a branch of the Protestant Church to start burning innocent women at the stake for being suspected of Witchcraft. The Jews have had their own introduction of "Reform" and the Muslims need to have their own "Reformation" if they are to avoid an all-out war with the rest of the world, which they will undoubtedly lose.

Many of the disciplines and punishments in today's Islam continue from their Judeo/Arab origins. Jews used to stone women to death for adultery, now they don't … but Muslims still do! We all remember the parable of Jesus: "He that is without sin, let him cast the first stone."

The Sunnis and the Shias came from the dilemma that Muhammed's sons had died and he had left only daughters.

43

Amongst the upper echelons of the Muslim community, arguments raged over his succession. Eventually, Umar Ibn al-Khattab, who was a senior, suggested that Abu Bakr would be the most suitable candidate as their leader. It was agreed, and Abu Bakr became Islam's first caliph (meaning supreme leader). This also confirmed Aisha's position. Not only was she a "Mother of the Believers" and favoured wife of the Holy Prophet, but she was also daughter of the first caliph of Islam.

The Sunni accepted Abu Bakr's nomination and election, but others, namely the Shia, believed that Muhammed had already chosen his successor in the form of his own son-in-law and cousin, Ali. They backed their argument by referring to a Hadith which says that Muhammed declared his intention in a speech at the pond of Khumm, three months before his death. Sunnis say that Muhammed merely meant that the believers should show Ali high regard and respect.

Thus began the blood-letting feud that continues to this very day.

Chapter 5

THE CALIPHATES, AND HIS MAJESTY'S PROTECTORATES

---◦⊙◦---

The first delineation of a caliphate was called the "Rashidun Caliphate." It spanned from 632 to 661 AD and it included four caliphs, referring to them as "the Rightly Guided ones," starting with Abu Bakr, Umar, Uthman, and finally Ali. Ali's appointment was an important step, because the Shia now regard Ali as their first caliph of Islam and they ignore the other three. The Sunni accept all four.

The remaining caliphates are as follows, but you will note that some overlap – the Abbasid Caliphate, for example, where in 945 AD Baghdad fell to the Buyid family dynasty, but then in 1258 AD the Mongols took control. The Abbasid Caliphate was then re-formed in Egypt under the Mamluks. In 1517 AD the Ottomans defeated the Mamluks and the caliphate was then centred in Istanbul.

(2)   The Umayyad Caliphate of Damascus. 661 – 750 AD

(3)   The Abbasid Caliphate. 750 – 945 / 1258 – 1517 AD

(4)   The Fatimid Caliphate. 909 – 1171 AD

(5)   The Umayyad Caliphate of Cordoba. 929 – 1031 AD

(6)   The Almohad Caliphate. 1147 – 1269 AD

(7) The Sokoto Caliphate of Nigeria. 1804 – 1903 AD

(8) The Ottoman Caliphate. 1517 – 1924 AD

(9) The Iran Khomeini Caliphate. 1979 –

(10) Dawn of the Final Caliphate. Tuesday, September 11th 2001 AD

Where do we go from here? First and foremost, we must face up to the reality of the situation and stop our politicians from continuing to be in denial. Stop apologising to the enemy in the hope that if we are nice to him, by adopting that old familiar Chamberlainesque formula, we shall awake in the morning and everything will be fine: It won't!

There are approximately 1.8 billion people in the world today who follow the religion founded by the Prophet Muhammed, and every last one of them believes in the absolute sanctity of his being. His every word, action, and deed on earth was perfect in the eyes of Allah, their God.

Of those 1.8 billion people, our security agencies within the English-speaking democracies estimate that approximately three hundred million of them, yes, that's 300 million, want to destroy our culture, butcher us to death in the most gruesome ancient biblical way, convert us to Islam, or force us to pay the jizya and accept the status of Dhimmi. That equates to an enemy equivalent in numbers to every man, woman, and child living in the United States of America today.

This enemy has declared war against us. He is without borders, without a defined territory, without any single race or ethnicity, and he is under no signed obligation to conform to any treaty of war or Geneva Convention. He kills wherever the opportunity arises to further his cause. He may dine with us, befriend us, or even send his children to the same school as us. Often he is brazen in his declaration of intent, and yet our political elite are more interested in massaging the truth and hiding the reality from the electorate.

Those are the cold-hard-facts that we must all face up to. Can we defend our freedom and our democratic values with minimal violence, and win? Of course we can! We must!

We begin by examining ourselves, and exactly what price we put on those freedoms and democratic values. President Ronald Reagan said it most eloquently:

> Freedom is never more than one generation away from extinction. We didn't pass it to our children in the bloodstream. It must be fought for, protected, and handed on for them to do the same, or one day we will spend our sunset years telling our children and our children's children what it was once like in the United States, where men were free.

As a boy growing up in England in the 1950s I was privileged enough to attend boarding school. Evidence of the Second World War was still everywhere to be seen, particularly in our cities. From the carriage window of the steam train on my way to school, I remember counting the Anderson bomb-shelters in the gardens of the houses as we passed them by.

I recall seeing the terrible bombsites of Manchester and Liverpool as if it were yesterday. Although our nation was on its knees both visibly and financially, nearly every city, every town, and every village started to erect cenotaphs to honour those who had surrendered their lives for our liberty, and to show them our eternal gratitude in stone, "Lest We Forget." We were one nation, bonded together with a clear identity, proud of our country's many accomplishments and its position in the world. We knew precisely the price of those freedoms and of those democratic values.

But what of us now?

Already, as I write, the leading left-wing activists within the Labour Party are stirring the youth, particularly in our universities, to rise up and help create a new totalitarian future for themselves. Democracy and the evils of capitalism go hand-in-hand, I hear them cry. Is History no longer a part of the curriculum? Is having the privilege of a higher education teaching them nothing?

For those of us who value our liberty and our democracy, this destructive march towards Cultural Marxism, and Antonio Gramsci's Critical Theory, should be deeply worrying to all of us. The German intellectual Socialists from the Frankfurt School of thought in the 1930s, quickly realised that Karl Marx was wrong, and that the workers didn't unite in the way that was originally intended. Society can only be truly controlled, when, first of all, you remove the glue that binds the traditional family together. When the family unit no longer has the father as its head, he being the main person that all the other members can turn to for protection, guidance, and love, the State steps in to become that father. The Church is already surrendering to this, and consequently, its influence is becoming more irrelevant by the day. The Cultural Marxist knows that you have to destroy a culture from within. These are the very same style thinkers who allied themselves to the Shia Islamist Clergy during the overthrow of the Shah of Iran. Their contribution was quickly and brutally dispensed with the minute that Khomeini took control. Totalitarians always give short measure to intellectuals; they are the first to go!

President Reagan's speech rings so true. The fight to preserve our liberty from the totalitarians doesn't end with the building of a cenotaph, it is ongoing and relentless. Nazism fell, Communism fell, and even the European Union was founded upon deceit. It led us to gratuitously surrender the sovereignty of our country to the control of an unelected European Commission. The totalitarians were at it again!

Jean Monnet, the founder of the European Union, said at the very beginning:

> Europe's nations should be guided towards the Super-State without their people understanding what is happening. This can be accomplished by successive steps, each disguised as having an economic purpose, but which will eventually, and irreversibly, lead to federation.

If you want to create "The Federal Union of European States," and thinly veneer it with the pretence of democracy, you must firstly dilute the deeply engrained individual and diverse identities of the Europeans. You can only do that with the encouragement of a mass movement of people and labour, an open-door policy! Follow that with an anthem, a flag and a single currency, and Hey Presto!

The problem is, Monnet didn't take into account that his open-door policy for Europe might just lead to allowing in a new type of totalitarian kid-on-the-block... Islam.

Suddenly, another new word was to appear in our English vocabulary. The word is jihad (meaning to strive). It was used in several contexts such as to strive to be more devout, or to be at war with one's inner weaknesses. It developed into meaning war against the non-believing Arab or the infidel crusader. Whenever it is uttered today it almost invariably means war against the disbeliever, the infidel, the kafir. Another word that we are less familiar with is the word riddah, which refers to "war against apostasy." I have previously stated that apostasy in Islam carries the death sentence, but what I failed to say was that it can also carry a similar sentence for any non-believer who tries to lead a Muslim astray or to assist him in abandoning his faith. So I say this advisedly: I would refrain from getting into any conversations about Islam whilst visiting a devoutly Muslim country. Such an accusation would be nigh-on impossible to deny in a Sharia court, where there is no Habeas Corpus, Magna Carta, or sympathetic jury to protect you.

As today's chaotic Islamic wars rage around the world, it is so often apostasy that justifies one Muslim to accuse another Muslim of failing to be a "True Muslim." This is bandied back and forth endlessly. The word takfir and the word kafir have a lot in common. A takfir is an impure Muslim, similar to the non-believer kafir; both are equally derogatory terms. The Saudi Arabian Wahhabi movement within the Sunni claim to adhere most closely to the life and commands of the Holy Prophet Muhammed, and therefore could never be accused of takfir. Likewise, the Shias of Iran and elsewhere also claim Islamic perfection, but n'er the twain shall meet.

Throughout the whole of Islamic history, the faithful have experienced a concatenation of ebbing and flowing, back and forth. Every so often a new Islamic purist arrives on the scene and starts to rein in those sections of Islam that he believes are straying too close to the ways of the infidel and threatening the order laid down by the Holy Prophet. You can't argue with a Mafia-style ideology. What he says is written there in the scriptures for all to see, and so it must be right.

The British, in building their vast empire, are probably the most experienced of all the infidels in dealing with jihad. In the Indian sub-continent, they interrupted the constant feuds between the Hindus and Muslims by advancing Christianity in their bid to Anglicise their empire. One such purist the British would meet along the way was Shah Waliullah Dehlawi (1703 – 1762). He believed the Indian Muslims needed to return fully to the ways of Muhammed and to eradicate foreign influences by force. Jihad, throughout the Islamic world, was starting to focus more on resistance to British and French colonialism. Other fundamentalists to appear include Muhammed Abd al Wahhab (1703 – 1792), the founder of Wahhabi Sunnis, and then later, in the 1830s, they would encounter Abd al-Qadir's resistance against them in Sudan.

Above all, Great Britain needed to protect her land trade routes to the Jewel in her Crown, India. It was therefore imperative that she had control of Central Asia and the Arabian Peninsula, not only to expand her imperial ambitions but to protect her against any possible Russian expansion. So far, they had always maintained good relations with the Turkish Ottoman caliph, the world's most powerful Islamic leader.

After the British aided the Ottomans in the Crimean War, fighting against the Russians in 1844, The Ottoman Empire had already begun its journey of decline. Its denouement came with the First World War when they made the mistake of joining forces with the Germans.

Countries such as Palestine, Jordan, Iraq, and Syria had been ruled by the Ottomans since 1517. The British appealed to them to join in the fight against the Ottoman/German alliance in return for guaranteed independence after a victorious war. However, behind the scenes, the British had other ideas.

In May of 1915, the British made a declaration to the Arabian people that despite the fact that the Ottomans had become their enemies, it in no way altered Great Britain's respect for Islam. We are all aware of the "Arab Revolt" and the part played in it by Lawrence of Arabia. But, of course, the British had no intention of granting independence. In addition to the protection of their overland trade routes, there was a new prize to be won. With the invention of the combustion engine, war had suddenly changed. The horse cavalry was no longer as effective. The invention of the new iron horse tank, and the motor vehicle, changed everything, and one thing the Arabian lands had plenty of was oil to fuel them. Instead of granting independent sovereignty, Great Britain appointed British advisors to administrate those countries. They were to become His Majesty's Protectorates.

What the British did do was to promise the then Meccan Sharif, Hussein Bin Ali, who claimed to be a descendant of Muhammed, that in return for leading the Arab Revolt, the British would then acknowledge him as the absolute ruler of the entire Arabian Peninsula. That would return the lands once conquered by Muhammed himself during his own lifetime to his descendant. Hussein would be the new caliph of all Islam. The British also promised to protect the holy Islamic sites of Mecca and Medina against any form of outside aggression. The plan was that, by bringing the caliphate back to the sacred sites of Arabia and away from Turkey, the British would be able to have a lot more control of the Arab world and Islam as a whole. Indeed, by doing that, it would appear that Britain was helping to restore Islam to its rightful place of worship.

However, the choice of Hussein was contrived, because they knew full well that his appointment would be controversial and would create disharmony within the Muslim world. The last thing the Brits wanted was to have a single caliph who could unite Islam into one Ummah Islamiyyah (meaning Universal Nation of Islam). Today, we would recognise that as the ambition of ISIS.

It was equally imperative to keep Islam divided then as it is now! Documents from the British Foreign Department of

India at the time said, "What we want is not a united Arabia, but a weak and disunited Arabia, split up into little principalities so far as possible under our suzerainty – but incapable of coordinated action against us, forming a buffer against the Powers in the West."

Hussein's efforts against the Ottomans proved fairly ineffectual, but after the First World War ended, he declared himself King of Arabia. The British only acknowledged his kingship as that of the area of Hijaz, which includes Mecca and Medina and part of the coastal section of Arabia. But, the Brits had another protégé up their sleeve, in the form of Abdul Aziz Ibn Saud. As predicted, confrontation ensued between Hussein and Saud. Saud had captured the Nejd region, including the city of Riyadh, and he was a formidable leader. The British government in India favoured Saud to be the champion, only because they believed that his aspirations were limited to the control of Arabia.

Hussein was a fairly orthodox Sunni, whereas Saud was a strict Islamist Wahhabi, which entails all of the brutality of Muhammed's reign of terror in the days of his conquests. Although a ceasefire was agreed in 1920, Saud continued relentlessly, and by the mid 1920s Hussein was defeated. The state of "Saudi Arabia" came into existence with the usual orgy of slaughter and butchery that follows the strict rule of adherence to Islamism. The control of Arabia was divided up amongst Saud's relatives, but the corruption of the then Saudi (now royal) family was described at the time as corrupt in the extreme. Said Aburish said of Saud that he was "a lecher and a bloodthirsty autocrat, whose savagery wreaked havoc across Arabia." Over 400,000 people lost their lives because Saud did not agree with the taking of prisoners. Several uprisings were lodged at the House of Saud only to result in mass killings, mostly of innocent civilians, women and children. A million people fled the country. In order to set an example, some 40,000 people were publicly executed, a practice that still goes on in Saudi Arabia today.

Chapter 6

CHURCHILL:
A VERY BRITISH VISIONARY

---◦◦◦---

By 1922, Winston Churchill was His Majesty's Colonial
Secretary, and he had considerable experience in dealing
with the Muslims. He increased Saud's subsidy to £100,000
per annum, which kept Saud sweet and the British as being
the major influence. The oil continued to flow but pretty
soon the giant American corporations were in control and
taking the lion's share.

On June 14th 1921, Churchill addressed the House of
Commons:

> The Wahhabis profess a life of exceeding austerity, and
> what they practice themselves they rigorously enforce
> on others. They hold it as an article of duty, as well as
> of faith, to kill all who do not share their opinions and
> to make slaves of their wives and children. Women
> have been put to death in Wahhabi villages for simply
> appearing in the streets. It is a penal offence to wear a
> silk garment. Men have been killed for smoking a
> cigarette, and as for alcohol, the most energetic
> supporter of the temperance cause in this country falls
> far behind them. Austere, intolerant, well armed and
> bloodthirsty, in their own regions the Wahhabis are a
> distinct factor that must be taken into account, and

they have been, and still are, very dangerous to the holy cities of Mecca and Medina, and to the whole institution of the pilgrimage, in which our Indian fellow-subjects are so deeply concerned ... The Emir Bin Saud has shown himself capable of leading and, within considerable limits, of controlling these formidable sectaries.

Churchill had first-hand knowledge of the Islamic mindset: He had fought them in both India and the Sudan as a young Officer in the British Army in 1897 and 1898.

Churchill's observations of the Islamic modus vivendi were equally as revealing then as they are today.

Of women's equal rights, he wrote:

The fact that in Muhammedan law every woman must belong to some man as his absolute property, either as a child, a wife, or as a concubine, must delay the final extinction of slavery until the faith of Islam has ceased to be a great power among men.

As he travelled throughout the Muslim countries, he made the following observation:

The effects are apparent in many countries: Improvident habits, slovenly systems of agriculture, sluggish methods of commerce and insecurity of property exist wherever the followers of the Prophet rule or live.

He further commented:

Individual Muslims may show splendid qualities, but the influence of the religion paralyses the social development of those who follow it. No stronger retrograde force exists in the world.

And finally, Churchill speaks from beyond the grave to those European Commissioners and their devotion to an open-door policy:

> Far from being moribund, Muhammedism is a militant and proselytizing faith. It has already spread throughout Central Africa, raising fearless warriors at every step, and were it not that Christianity is sheltered in the strong arms of science, the science against which it [Islam] has vainly struggled, the civilisation of modern Europe might fall, as fell the civilisation of ancient Rome.

Churchill was not alone amongst British politicians to have strong views on the subject of Islam. Gladstone, before him, once raised a copy the Qur'an high in the air at a speech in the House of Commons and declared, "So long as there is this book, there will be no peace in the world."

The Ikhwan (meaning brethren) had been Saud's principal military force, and were responsible for the defeat of Hussein. They were mostly made up of converted Bedouin tribes who had embraced the strict Wahhabi doctrine. Some started to be discontent with Saud's close relationship with the British, and the influence they had over him (possibly that old takfir thing lurking below the surface?).

Saud had relegated Ikhwanis during relative peacetime, thanks to the presence of a British military force, to the job of educators and monitors of social and moral standards (religious police). They were to metamorphose into the Mujahideen, a name we are very familiar with today.

Time and time again, the purists keep rising up wherever and whenever a religious apathy sets in somewhere in the world. Abdul A'la Mawdudi (1903 – 1979), an Indian Islamist academic, founded the Jamaat-e-Islami, which was later to become the largest Islamic organisation in Asia. His efforts resulted in the separation of Muslim Pakistan from Hindu and Buddhist India. And so, yet again, the quest for world domination by conversion and politicisation takes one more step forward. False Islamic leaders of the twentieth century needed to be forcibly replaced or reminded of their duty to Allah and His Messenger.

1979 was a pivotal year: Not only did it see the successful Khomeini caliphate in Iran, but it also marked the invasion of Afghanistan by the Russians. There was little persuading required in order to whip up a frenzy of religious fervour against the godless Russian infidels.

Abdullah Yusuf Azzam (1941 – 1989) was a Jordanian cleric and a Doctor in Islamic studies, who propagated the seeds of the modern form of jihad that we are all, sadly, experiencing today in New York, Paris, London, Manchester, and others. Azzam travelled throughout those countries speaking at mosques and inciting the believers to take up arms and travel to join the Mujahideen in the mountains of Afghanistan. The mosques of Great Britain, France, and elsewhere became a hotbed for recruitment. He inspired young men throughout the entire West, including visiting over 50 cities in the United States. He preached to mosques filled with testosterone-loaded youths, telling them tales of the acts of immense bravery being committed by their Mujahideen brothers. They learned of miracles being performed against the infidel Russians, and how their sacrifice would reap them untold rewards of virgins, and a guaranteed place in paradise.

Azzam declared a fatwa in defence of the Muslim lands. In it, he said:

> If a piece of Muslim land the size of a hand-span is infringed upon, then jihad becomes a personal obligation on every Muslim male and female, where the child shall march forward without the permission of its parents and the wife without permission of the husband.

What today's political appeasers in the West do not seem to be able to grasp is the idea that in the eyes of the true Muslim, once a territory comes under Islamic control, whether it be a country, a town, or a village, in any country of the world, from that moment forward, it can never be classed as anything but the property of Allah and His Messenger. If for whatever reason it is lost, at some point in the future, it must be returned by whatever means possible. If not by force, then by stealth, political infiltration, and subversion. If you fail to learn that fact, then it shall be at your own peril, or that of your children.

The United States, in particular, plunged headfirst into assisting the Mujahideen with their holy war against the Soviet Union. The Americans admired Azzam's rallying cries and his ability to recruit a powerful fighting force from around the world, under the brotherhood of a religious belief only. Little did they realise that he would become the "Father of Global Jihad" only for it to be turned against them, and the rest of us. In a television documentary in America called *Terrorists Among Us: Jihad in America* he instructs his followers to wage jihad in the United States. He often explained openly that "those that believe that Islam can flourish and can be victorious without Jihad, fighting and blood are deluded and have no understanding of this religion."

In the fight in Afghanistan, Azzam had called upon Osama Bin Laden to join him. Bin Laden was the son of a billionaire Saudi family who had close connections with the king. He also was university educated, and, standing at 6 feet 5 inches tall, he made an imposing and charismatic biblical figure. His interests included reading about Field Marshal Bernard Montgomery, and writing poetry. He was also a keen supporter of Arsenal Football Club.

By May of 1988, the Russians had had enough. The Russian people were comparing Afghanistan to the Americans' Vietnam War and Mikhail Gorbachev decided to pull the plug on it and withdraw his troops. The Russian economy just couldn't continue to carry the burden of it for even one more day.

Azzam and Bin Laden rejoiced in victory and re-branded the Mujahideen as al-Qaeda, (meaning the base, or the foundation). The faithful from around the world believed that such a victory could only have happened with the divine intervention of Allah himself. Just as with the Holy

Prophet at the Battle of Badr, Allah had sent his army of invisible angels to help the Mujahideen. How else could a small army of fighting men defeat a giant superpower like Russia?

The casualties among the early rookie recruits were considerable, with only about 55,000 fighting men still left standing after the Russians left.

Azzam and Bin Laden now had a seriously experienced fighting force at their disposal, but with no one to fight. Azzam urged the creation of vanguard cells of jihad be set up around the world, primarily in the existing mosques and centres of Islamic study:

> This vanguard constitutes the solid qaeda for the hoped-for society. We shall continue the jihad no matter how long the way, until the last breath and the last beat of the pulse – or, until we see the Islamic State established.

Extremist cells were, and are, being created, not only in America, Canada, Australia, and the crusader countries of Great Britain and Europe, but also in Chechnya, the Philippines, Malaysia, Thailand, Bosnia, Somalia, Sudan, Nigeria, Eritrea, and Spain.

Spain is an Islamic fundamentalist's must have, as far as reclaiming former Islamic land is concerned (after the humiliation of starting the Islamisation of Spain, from the Moorish invasion of 711 AD to the total expulsion of Islam by 1492 AD when Spain successfully returned to being an all Catholic Christian country). The celebration of that final expulsion still happens every year in Spain today, it is simply known as the "Festival of the Moors and the Christians."

With the rise of each extreme caliphate-seeker comes a hailstorm of opposition from rival groups, and Azzam was to be no exception. As a Sunni Palestinian, he believed that the epicentre of jihad should spiral out from Palestine, and that he could train his Palestinian Hammas fighters in Afghanistan and Pakistan in order to keep a constant flow of them chipping away at the destruction of Israel. Hammas had only been recently formed, in 1987, as an offshoot of the Egyptian Muslim Brotherhood. Palestine had other figures to contend with, including Yasser Arafat, head of the PLO (Palestine Liberation Organisation). Arafat was the most high-profile political figure to be involved in a series of so-called peace agreements, which would involve the creation of separate independent nation-states of Palestine and Israel. Laughably, he received the Nobel Peace Prize. After one such agreement he was criticised by his fellow Muslims for being too flexible in allowing the Jews to have the upper hand. He was overheard saying, "remember Hudaybiyyah," which referred to Muhammed's deceit of the Meccans by breaching the ten-year treaty. They knew exactly what he meant by that, but an infidel wouldn't.

One cannot mention modern-day caliphate-seeking luminaries without referring to the name Sayyid Qutb, 1906 – 1966. He was member of the Muslim Brotherhood and a spiritual mentor to Azzam, but he was hanged for plotting to kill President Nasser of Egypt. Although Qutb often wore a suit and tie and had all the outward appearance of a

Westerner, he was nonetheless a confirmed Islamist. He believed Nasser was a takfirist and not a true Muslim. President Nasser had publicly mocked the idea that women should be forced to wear the hijab and he also enjoyed the trappings of the decadent modern world.

I think I'm safe in saying that the trilogy of modern-day world jihad has got to be Qutb, Azzam, and Bin Laden.

In 1989 a first attempt was made on Azzam's life when a bomb that was placed under the pulpit that he was speaking from failed to explode. The second attempt was successful: His car drove over an explosive devise hidden under a street in Peshawar, Pakistan. Nobody seemed to take responsibility, but every man and his dog was blamed, from the Jordanian intelligence, Iranian intelligence, CIA, MI6, to the Jews and even Osama Bin Laden himself. Bin Laden and Azzam had previously argued about where to train future jihadi fighters. Bin Laden wanted to do it through the numerous cells being set up around the world, whereas Azzam wanted to keep it concentrated in Afghanistan and to send his fully prepared martyrs out from there. His prime objective, though, was Israel. If you cripple Israel then that would be the greatest rallying call of all to the brothers and sisters in Islam for a world jihad.

Following Azzam's death, Osama Bin Laden was the uncontested heir apparent. He still had his 55,000 troops, ready, able, waiting, and willing. So he went to see his old family friend, the Saudi king, and offered his services in getting rid of Iraq's Saddam Hussein. But the king was having nothing to do with it.

Undoubtedly, His Majesty could see the difficulties in employing a maverick like Bin Laden, who was so televisual and charismatic and was already being recognised worldwide as a kind of cult figure, and potentially a new Supreme Caliph. There was every possibility Bin Laden could become so immensely powerful he may even eventually turn on the Saudis. Much as the king needed to get rid of Hussein, because of his invasion of Kuwait in August of 1990, instead, he decided to make Bin Laden stateless by removing his Saudi citizenship, and to leave Hussein for the West to deal with.

The king even allowed Allied troops onto Saudi soil in order to prevent Hussein from turning his attentions against Saudi Arabia. This was the greatest sacrilege of all. No foreign infidel troops had ever been allowed to set their dirty crusader's boots on the precious soil of the holy sites of Mecca and Medina before, never mind at the invitation of the king himself. This was the final straw, the ultimate betrayal against the Holy Prophet, as far as Bin Laden was concerned.

Now it was even more important for him to change history and to bring the war to the infidel's doorstep. The whole concept of war was about to change. It was no longer a simple question of territorial warfare requiring a military strategy. That old rulebook needed throwing in the bin.

Chapter 7

OSAMA BIN LADEN, AND THE TWIN TOWERS

―∘⊙⊙∘―

So far, conflicts had been about the systematic gain or loss of territory, with the ultimate reward being the acquisition of land or a change of regime. The rules of war had always complied with a mathematical formula, a chess game. Each new war leader could refer to previously written textbooks, authored by the Athenians or the Caesars, Napoleon Bonaparte, Rommel, and Montgomery. War had always followed an element of gentlemanly procedure, requiring certain rules.

General Norman Schwarzkopf, the United States Commander of Allied forces in the Iraq war, with 750,000 men under his command, had been a cadet at West Point Academy. He was an avid reader of all such great military strategists. He admitted that in the Iraq war he had meticulously followed, in finite detail, the battle line formula first implemented by Alexander the Great: It worked! And his Allied invasion was successful.

Osama Bin Laden was about to change all of that. He was far more interested in emulating two of the greatest war strategists in the history of the world: The founders of a) the Mogul Empire, Genghis Khan, and b) the Islamic Empire, Muhammed. They both employed the same tactics of advanced "terror." To inflict such absolute brutality on the enemy and his family, you have to make the vision of war so utterly gruesome. Behead them, burn them alive, bury them, crucify them and quarter their children in front of as many witnesses as possible. Once you have destroyed his mindset to resist, and his will to fight, then your enemy will yield as submissively as the lamb to the slaughter. "Fear!" is the greatest component of all. And Osama Bin Laden was about to be able to achieve that in a way that Genghis Khan and Muhammed could only dream of.

Hitler had tried it before him, with his Blitzkrieg bombings of innocent civilians in London, partly in the hope that it would terrify the general populace and demoralise British frontline troops, knowing that their loved ones back home were being slaughtered: It failed. In that particular case, it had the opposite effect. The civilians mounted their own defences and felt they were fighting the common enemy shoulder-to-shoulder alongside their own boys, who were doing the same overseas. When Buckingham Palace was hit by a bomb and their Queen said, "Now, I feel that I can look the Eastenders in the eye," it cemented national fervour to an even stronger level of resistance.

No, Osama Bin Laden's war was to be very different.

A publishing house, with internet site, was set up in London – called Azzam Publications. It started to churn out paramilitary literature and glamorous recruitment videos. The infrastructure for its release was already in place in the mosques around the globe. That site was to be closed down, but not before a virus of mimic sites began to spread from extremist cells and from the privacy of young men's bedrooms around the world.

Winston Churchill's comment "Christianity is sheltered in the strong arms of science, the science against which Islam has vainly struggled" – suddenly, that no longer applied. Science in the form of the internet was about to be the Islamist's greatest weapon of war. It is the most potent vehicle for recruitment and shock tactic propaganda ever conceived by man. You could behead an innocent American journalist whilst putting it on the internet, and within a few seconds billions of people around the world could view it and reel back in horror, and fear!

On September 11th 2001 in New York City, it was a gloriously sunny Tuesday morning when two fully loaded passenger planes, American Airlines flight 11 and United Airlines flight 175, were deliberately flown into the Twin Towers. Within one hour and forty-two minutes, both towers had collapsed. 2,996 people were killed. Over 6,000 were injured. 343 firefighters lost their lives, along with 72 police officers. Two further flights from the same two airlines also crashed: one into the Pentagon and another into a field, which was only due to the passengers attempting to fight back against the hijackers.

Shortly before their collapse, the images of the World Trade Centre Twin Towers, both burning and smoking, were instantly beamed around the world, with viewing figures of up into the billions. Every worldwide spectator was about to witness the two most iconic edifices of capitalism come crashing down.

Nearly everyone on the planet reacted with the same feelings of absolute horror, sympathy, revulsion, tears, and confusion ... but not everyone. In Islamic countries everywhere, there was cause for great celebration. Even in tiny pockets of Great Britain and Europe we witnessed dancing and laughter.

The Dawn of the Final Caliphate had truly begun.

Our security information tells us that somewhere in the region of 17% of the entire Islamic world of some 1.8 billion people had just officially declared war on infidels everywhere. It had taken only 19 of them to bring down the Twin Towers.

Not all of them have access to the sophisticated weaponry needed to carry out major atrocities but, nonetheless, all are still openly at war with us. In addition to that, a huge percentage will have silent leanings of sympathy to the cause and, in some cases, collaboration. They have no choice: Indoctrination, and rules within their religion, demands it. And that is an undeniable fact that must be faced by all of us.

In December, three months after the fall of the Twin Towers, Bin Laden released a video. In it he said:

> It has become clear that the West in general and America in particular have an unspeakable hatred for Islam ... It is the hatred of crusaders. Terrorism against America deserves to be praised because it was a response to injustice, aimed at forcing America to stop its support for Israel, which kills our people ... We say that the end of the United States is imminent whether Bin Laden or

his followers are alive or dead, for the awakening of the Muslim Ummah [meaning single Islamic State or community] has occurred.

Osama Bin Laden's al-Qaeda admitted responsibility for the towers disaster. The message being churned out from then on, in internet videos and propaganda literature worldwide, was to be aimed primarily at the young and the gullible. The message was that jihad is not the exclusive domain of the paid soldier but the duty of every Muslim who wants to please Allah. Those that don't are the hypocrites, the apostates, and the takfir. The process of metamorphosis was to take Islamic extremism from Mujahideen and al-Qaeda along with numerous offshoots like Boko Haram in Nigeria, which was also taking hold in Cameroon, to Niger and even Mali and Chad. The Taliban continued to wage war in Afghanistan until Allied forces mostly destroyed them – but not before their fear tactics of demanding total obedience to Sharia, with a price tag of staggering brutality, became legendary.

The Taliban received its funding not only through plunder, extortion, theft, and taxation, but also through a powerful paymaster. In the year 2000, the Human Rights Watch issued the following statement:

Of all the foreign powers involved in efforts to sustain and manipulate the ongoing fighting in Afghanistan, Pakistan is distinguished both by the sweep of its objectives and the scale of its efforts, which include soliciting for the Taliban, bankrolling Taliban operations, providing diplomatic support as the

Taliban's virtual emissaries abroad, arranging training for Taliban fighters, recruiting skilled and unskilled manpower to serve in Taliban armies, planning and directing offensives, providing and facilitating shipments of ammunition and fuel, and directly providing combat support.

I have no doubt that the Taliban are presently re-branding themselves, whilst quietly biding their time. In the meantime, Prime Minister Theresa May insists on continuing the legacy of David Cameron by increasing the British foreign aid budget to Pakistan by adding another £100 million to it, bringing it to £441 million for the year 2017. In reply, Pakistan has announced a huge increase in its arms budget, including a new fleet of submarines. It spends £20 million per annum on an utterly ludicrous space project. It is also one of the world's very few nuclear powers. Each and every British taxpayer pays £360 per annum towards the £13 billion foreign aid budget. Less than 1% of the entire population of Pakistan pays any tax at all. Pakistan is one of the most corrupt countries on earth. It is a breeding ground for the most dedicated supporters of world jihad and anti-West hate propaganda. But the British government insists that the money is going to those poorest of people who are most in need!

On May 2nd 2011, "Operation Neptune Spear" took place at 1 a.m. The US Navy SEALS successfully raided a compound house in Abbottabad, Pakistan, killing Osama Bin Laden.

A former Pakistani intelligence officer had offered the Americans details of Bin Laden's whereabouts in exchange for $25 million. Whilst the entire civilised world was looking for him, Pakistani intelligence services had been holding Bin Laden in this safe-house since 2006. Pakistan was keeping him in order to better manage their very complex relationships with numerous Pakistani and Afghan Islamist organisations. The safe-house was located within a stone's throw of one of the country's major military and intelligence centres.

It is confirmed that Saudi Arabia was paying for his board and lodgings, so-to-speak. But, of course, the Pakistani government had no knowledge of it. Surveys carried out after the death of Bin Laden showed that two thirds of the entire Islamic community worldwide were either outraged at, or at least disagreed with, his killing: Millions of them vowed revenge. It has to be said that several Western organisations such as Amnesty International also objected to his killing. You couldn't make it up!

Chapter 8

ABU BAKR AL-BAGHDADI, AND THE BIRTH OF ISIL

———•᎐⊙⊙᎐•———

There are more parochial Islamist groups that have been sprouting up elsewhere in the world: Al Shabaab, for example. Based in Somalia, it linked itself to al-Qaeda and engaged in conflict against the Federal Government of Somalia, who were considered the enemies of Islam. For a while, Al Shabaab had a thriving business in piracy on the high seas off the Horn of Africa, by attacking container ships and demanding multi-million dollar ransoms. Somali Al Shabaab fundraising and recruitment agencies have been uncovered in both the United States and Great Britain, but in 2014 an American drone managed to send their leader, Moktar Ali Zubeyr, to an early grave.

I'm afraid there is no way of sugar-coating the fact that Islamic fundamentalism is the greatest threat to this, the modern, libertarian, democratic civilisation that our forefathers fought so hard to preserve, and we have thus far continued to enjoy.

Like all totalitarian ideologies, Islam removes the freedom from the individual. It demands total obedience and subservience in all the facets of his life. It is a far greater threat even than Communism was at the time of the Cuban missile crisis. Then, we knew precisely who our enemy was. Now, we face our very first trans-regional insurgency, where the enemy can be your next door neighbour or your friend.

Taqiyya (meaning prudence or fear) is another word to recently enter our English vocabulary. The origin of the word was such that a Shia Muslim was permitted to lie to a Sunni Muslim if he thought that his life was in danger. This was also adopted more widely by the Sunnis to mean that any Muslim was given permission to lie or cheat if he genuinely thought that either he, or Islam, was being endangered by an infidel. Over time, the word has become more loosely adopted by most Muslims to mean that he can always lie to an infidel if it is to his own advantage (as Arafat did over the Treaties he signed with Israel).

Sami Makarem, a prominent Lebanese Islamic scholar, wrote *Al Taqiyya Fi Al-Islam* (*Dissimulation in Islam*). In it, he said:

> Taqiyya is of fundamental importance in Islam. Practically every Islamic sect agrees to it, and practices it. We can go so far as to say that the practice of Taqiyya is mainstream in Islam, and that those few sects not practicing it diverge from the mainstream. Taqiyya is very prevalent in Islamic politics, especially in the modern era.

No sooner does the West remove one malignant tumour than the X-ray shows that another one has popped up in a totally different place. Following the removal of Osama Bin Laden, we then started to hear the name Abu Bakr al-Baghdadi. Baghdadi had changed his name from Ibrahim Awad Ibrahim al-Badri; it is obvious that he wanted to associate himself with Abu Bakr, the first caliph of Islam and a man closest to Muhammed.

Baghdadi was reputed to be a quiet, shy, insular man who started to preach from the pulpit. There is no doubt that he was an inspirational speaker, and before the West knew too much about him he became head of a new group known as the Islamic State of Iraq and the Levant (ISIL). He also had attained a doctorate degree in Islamic studies. The Islamic State of Iraq had been an offshoot division of al-Qaeda, and when its leader, Abu Omar al-Baghdadi, was killed, the latest Abu Bakr al-Baghdadi was elected leader.

Immediately following the death of Osama Bin Laden, Baghdadi made a public announcement praising Bin Laden and promising revenge for his death. There followed a wave of ISIL suicide bombings, IEDs (improvised explosive devices), and light arms attacks, which killed around 200 people in Baghdad alone. This happened within days of the American withdrawal of its troops. Baghdadi's ISIL turned its immediate attention to the Shia Mahdi Army, run by a Shia warlord called Muqtadi Al Sadr, whom Baghdadi referred to as "the filthy ones of the Dar Al Dajjal" (meaning the House of Liars, and Deceivers).

The Muslim faith places everyone into a "House." You are either in the Dar al-Islam, which is an Islamic place under complete Islamic control and therefore a "House of Peace," or you are in a Dar al-Harb, which is a "House of War." Prior to the bringing down of the Twin Towers, the United States, Great Britain, and their allies were sometimes referred to as Dar al-Kufr, the "House of Heathens" or, Dar al-Gharb, the "House of the West."

All Western countries are now most definitely referred to as Dar al-Harb. However, as the Muslim communities continue to multiply and take possession of the towns and areas in those Western countries, once they hold not only numeric superiority but also the political control of the local councils, they then are considered Dar al-Islam. They can never again be referred to as Dar al-Gharb because for evermore, those towns belong to Allah and His Messenger.

Western politicians, in particular, cannot seem to understand this aspect of Islam, and they continue to blindly delude themselves that the imams will eventually come round to embracing integration and we will all live happily ever after, like in some Hippie commune.

This is totally impossible! Islam cannot integrate with anyone without a modern "Reformation".

There is no compromise! Their extreme scriptures strictly forbid it!

With the greatest of kindly intentions, our clergy, our teachers and our Cub-Scout Akelas may reach out their hand of friendship to the local mosques, and indeed they will receive smiles, promises, and sweet encouraging platitudes in return. The imams will even invite school children from the local Anglican church to come and visit the mosque to show them how Muslims pray. The children are then invited to join in, in friendly imitation. But no such encouragement is reciprocated by the Muslim children. There will always be an excuse to decline.

You must understand that deep rooted behind every smile is

the caliphate. It is the one and only purpose of Islam to purify the world under Islam, and to bring the world to Islam, in order that all may receive the blessings of Allah before the final judgement.

Of that there is no compromise, whether it be conversion by gentle persuasion, by force, or by death, for those who flatly refuse to accept it. These are the indisputable facts of the Islamic doctrine.

Imams and ordinary Muslims may seem hesitant or slightly embarrassed when confronted by such questions from an unbeliever; they will immediately quote early scriptures from the Meccan section of the Qur'an, in order to offer them reassurance and to send the unbeliever merrily on their way.

The declaration of the intention to re-establish the caliphate came as early as 1924, when Ataturk dismissed the caliph with his attempt to bring Turkey into the modern world and to offer it a more Western way of life. Millions of Muslims vowed then to rid the world of those false Muslims who they felt were corrupted by the heretical values offered to them by the infidel.

For the next 50 years Islam remained a ship without a rudder, inflicting mostly minor insurgencies around the world. The Iran uprising localised the new caliphate and brought it to the world's attention. That is, until 9/11 changed everything.

Another important name to mention is that of Dr. Ayman al-Zawahiri, an Egyptian physician from Cairo. He had been the doctor attending to the wounded Mujahideen fighters in

Afghanistan and had become a close friend of Bin Laden whilst they were both there.

Under a pseudonym, and relying on his doctoral credentials, he even travelled to California, where he gave talks in several of the mosques there. He was theoretically on a fundraising mission on behalf of Red Crescent Hospitals (Muslim equivalent to the Red Cross), raising money for Afghan children who had been blown up and disfigured by Russian landmines. His California tour raised $2,000 in total.

It is now widely accepted that Dr. al-Zawahiri was the real brains when it came to all the very serious worldwide al-Qaeda attacks, and Bin Laden was more the frontman, because he looked the part. Zawahiri exploited the internet and engaged online with Muslims around the world to encourage and support them with their most noble work of promoting global jihad.

Upon learning of a "non-violence initiative" being organised in his home country of Egypt against the jihadi terror campaign, he was so incensed with rage at the apparent surrender of the cause that he arranged for the massacre of tourists at the Temple of Hatshetsut. Six of his men dressed as police officers machine-gunned and hacked to death 58 tourists, including six newly married Japanese couples all on their honeymoon. The Egyptian tourist industry virtually collapsed for several years after that, and there was such a backlash that he tried to blame the police. He then blamed the tourists, saying it was their own fault for coming to Egypt in the first place. The Egyptian judiciary sentenced him to death, in absentia. He continues to be the leader of al-Qaeda and continues to spread the message of holy war.

It is interesting to note that Japan does not have a problem with Islam. Japan does not allow Muslims citizenship or permanent residency. Japan does not allow the Qur'an to be published in Arabic.

Japan does not allow the propagation of Islam in its country.

Japan has surveillance on all Muslims and Sharia law is banned.

Japan does not allow Muslims to rent a house.

Japan considers all Muslims to be fundamentalists.

In Zawahiri's publication *Knights Under the Prophet's Banner*, which is also known as *Warriors Under the Flag of Muhammed*, the doctor makes it very clear that this is the final journey, the push toward the judgement where all human beings must submit to jihad or be destroyed. Victory over the disbelievers is inevitable, it says. The Mujahideen in Afghanistan proved that against the Russians, when only a year after they were beaten back by the brave warriors of the holy war, the Soviet Union superpower collapsed. This was surely the will of Allah. America and her remaining minor superpowers will follow soon. Every man, woman, and child must now choose to be blessed by living in the house of Dar al-Islam, or be cursed and die in the house of Dar al-Harb.

Zawahiri's social media propaganda machine continues to move on relentlessly. YouTube videos show, in graphic detail, beheadings, crucifixions, people being burnt alive and stoned to death. Muhammed had to rely on word of mouth to deliver such terror tactics as his strategy of war.

Zawahiri can deliver the message to every computer and mobile phone around the world in seconds. His battle cry and call-to-arms has no ethnic division, no national bounderies, no age limit. It is a brotherhood of the mind and of the soul.

These propaganda videos are of such a high standard of cinematography and so cleverly composed and edited, Joseph Goebbels would be green with envy. To young men everywhere, there is a certain glamour attached to seeing warriors fully clothed in black with their faces obscured. It was the same attraction to that fearsome all-black uniform that prompted young men to aspire to join the Hitler SS. The SS uniform was superbly designed by Hugo Boss to combine both glamour and fear. It's why S.W.A.T. teams don't wear pink!

To add fuel to an already raging bush-fire of Islamic turmoil, in Syria the al-Nusra Front, (Jabhat al-Nusra) a Wahhabi extremist group, and accepted as the Syrian branch of al-Qaeda, was also busy building on its jihadi uprising against the Syrian government, led by President Bashar Hafez al-Assad (yet another medical doctor). His father, Hafez al-Assad, had been President from 1971 to 2000, and within a month of his father's death, Bashar Assad was elected President by a 99.7% referendum approval. In 2007, a second referendum was enacted where he received 97.6% and in 2014 in a contested election, he won with 88.7%.

Some Western allies and the European Commissioners (that's those very same unelected European Commissioners we are talking about) declared the Syrian election a sham!

And yet, a totally independent international delegation of observers confirmed that the election was, indeed, both fair and free. The West had previously always viewed Assad as a modern-day reformer with an English wife, and his government referred to themselves as secularists. However, in the civil war that Assad was conducting against the jihadi al-Nusra Front, Assad was accused of being implicated in war crimes. The Arab League, which includes Saudi Arabia, Yemen, and Iraq, plus America and the EU, all the countries with impeccable records of purity and integrity, demanded the immediate resignation of Assad. He flatly refused and said the allegations were false. Assad rebuked America in particular for leading the intervention against a democratically elected president in order to change the regime, and so he sought help elsewhere, and received it, from Vladimir Putin.

Just to complicate things even more, al-Baghdadi and his ISIL forces demanded that the al-Nusra Front amalgamate with them as one unit in the effort to bring Syria into the Islamic State. The leaders of the al-Nusra Front refused, and then sought help from al-Qaeda's Dr. Zawahiri, who recommended that al-Baghdadi's ISIL should be abolished. Zawahiri's judgement was that al-Baghdadi should concentrate his efforts in Iraq, not Syria. In response, al-Baghdadi took control of the vast majority of al-Nusra's troops.

President Assad was not completely alone, with only the Russians standing by his side. The Lebanese Shia fighters, called Hezbollah, were also on board. They were bitter rivals of the al-Nusra Front and were more than willing to help

Assad. The main reason was probably that they didn't want any of the Syrian conflict spilling over into Lebanon. Their principal hatred was for the Jews and Israel. And then there's the Free Syrian Army to deal with as well. They are breakaways from the government's official Syrian Army and they are fighting against President Assad also. Then you've got President Trump who bombs the airport and the British saying they might have to throw their hat into the ring also.

Are you still keeping up with me, or have I lost you?

Perhaps only now are you are beginning to realise the immense complexity of the problem that faces our world today.

Whereas, only a few years ago, like me, you more than likely had only ever heard that Sunni Muslims have an issue with Shia Muslims, and both of them have an issue with us. But quite frankly, it was too far away to be bothered about, and you didn't really care about it anyway. 9/11 changed all that – not only for the Americans, but for all of us.

Chapter 9

AL-BAGHDADI DECLARES HIMSELF THE NEW SUPREME CALIPH

───◦⊙◦───

In June of 2014, al-Baghdadi declared a new World Caliphate, with himself as Supreme Caliph. He was to be referred to from then on as Caliph Ibrahim. The Islamic scholars around the world agreed and disagreed as to his legitimacy, with many of them saying that he failed to meet the criteria on several points and that his caliph status was invalid.

The Nigerian Boko Haram immediately accepted al-Baghdadi as their Supreme Caliph and declared Bayat (meaning an oath of allegiance) and more than a dozen Islamic fundamentalist organisations around the world followed suit. Now he had a serious fighting force, a globally interconnected terrorist infrastructure was beginning to take shape for the first time in history.

Baghdadi upped his operations in Syria. This was important as a geographic location. ISIL was to become ISIS (Islamic State of Iraq and Syria), because northern Syria is the final place of "al-Shaam," the Islamic place for the final Judgement Day ... Armageddon.

The Prophet Muhammed had said, "Al-Shaam is the land of the gathering, and of the resurrection."

The Jews and the Christians believe that the final Day of Judgement will take place in northern Israel and not in Syria, so it looks like if that day comes soon, then there will be a considerable amount of confusion and a great many disappointments.

Now that there appears to be some form of unified structure for the fundamentalist caliphateers to hitch their wagon to, the social media recruitment campaign has become even more sophisticated. They all believe that the Judgement Day is nigh, and so al-Baghdadi has been turning the heat up on calling the young people from around the world to come and fight the final battles against the infidel, as directed by the holy scriptures.

The latest directive to those unable to travel, or who have restricted funds, is that they can still receive the highest blessings from Allah by their martyrdom within the countries that they live in.

As long as they kill by whatever means, and create terror in the hearts of the unbelievers, then their blessings will be bountiful. This is why we have recently started to see a spate of low-cost killings using knives, machetes, or car and van attacks. Not that there is any shortage of money: ISIS is the richest terrorist organisation ever to have been recorded. It is estimated that it has a GDP (gross domestic product) of around $500,000,000 per annum. Its criminal activities are beyond belief, separate from clearing every bank wherever it goes. It stole $800 million from the Iraqi government alone. Then there are the sales of priceless antiquities plundered from captured towns. It used to just blow them up until it realised that there was a huge market out there for stolen antiques. Then there is the extortion business, drugs money, ransom for kidnappings, and the list goes on and on.

Following in the jet-stream of Bin Laden's glory, Baghdadi has achieved far greater success at branding the caliphate and the jihad as marketable products than Bin Laden or Zawahiri ever could.

Gullible young Muslims throughout the world now don't even need to be part of an ISIS cell in order to receive their passport to Allah's blessings and the virgins in paradise who await them. Before, they had required authority and training, because suicide bombers need sophisticated equipment and an ability to permanently try to outwit the security services. Martyrs need to keep a vow of silence, lest they unwittingly betray their fellow brethren in this, the holy war.

Now, you can simply hire a car and kill as many people as possible whilst shouting "Allahu Akbar." That will get you on the front cover of every media outlet. Not only do you get all of your heavenly blessings, and most likely you will die from a policeman's bullet, but you will also get the admiration of your peers from around the world, who will then want to emulate your actions. The simple fact is that in a few weeks' time no one will ever remember you again, except possibly your mother.

Baghdadi has also encouraged the employment of talent spotters, to infiltrate the mosques and the seats of learning, from the Islamic schools in the West to universities everywhere, where they seek out vulnerable candidates as potential martyrs and activists.

Although many of the Arab states and Islamic scholars refuse to accept Baghdadi as the latest caliph, nonetheless he has succeeded in going some way towards fulfilling the scriptural doctrine of the caliphate, whereas so far, they have all failed. He accuses them of being more interested in the pleasures of this life, rather than their duty to the next.

I beg all of those men and women who govern us today in the West. To you, I say this: "Do not underestimate the huge significance of Baghdadi's re-establishment of the World Caliphate, where its sole aim is the eventual abolition of the individual state, and the unification of all nations under a single Islamic banner. All men are ruled by the law of Sharia and the Holy Qur'an must be their Constitution."

Remember, the caliphate existed for more than a thousand years, until Ataturk put an end to it. Millions upon millions of Muslims were deeply embittered by its abolition then, and their grandchildren are being taught of it with the same embitterment today. Baghdadi has given them a new and revived hope, and that is not going to go away any time soon.

What is so deeply disturbing is the constant denial by the Western leadership that there is a problem. Immediately after the Manchester bombing, the newly elected Mayor and former Member of Parliament Andy Burnham said of the bomber, "This man wasn't a Muslim, he was a terrorist. This was an act of extremism, it doesn't represent any religion, it doesn't represent any community."

The idiocy of such a remark beggars belief. Time after time, we keep seeing our politicians cower like beaten dogs at the very thought of making an honest critical comment about the current perpetrator of the most heinous crime. The first port-of-call by the authorities is to explore the possibility that the perpetrator was mentally disturbed, even when witnesses say that he was shouting "Allahu Akbar" at the time of the crime.

Manchester bomber Salman Abedi was born and bred in Manchester. He had attended Salford University and worshipped at the Didsbury Mosque. Immediately after he had just slaughtered 22 innocent concert-goers, naturally the mosque wanted to disassociate itself from any responsibility of influence. On a television interview, the elders and imams displayed all the oleaginous qualities of snake-oil salesmen. It was subsequently discovered that many of the worshippers there had been fighters in the Libyan Civil War against Gaddafi. The imam himself, Mostafa Abdullah Graf, was seen on a video wearing full battle fatigues, loading ammunition. On AFP TV, he says: "Thank Allah everything is ready, we are just waiting for the attack!" This holy man of God and ambassador for the "religion of peace" told the *Manchester Evening News* that he had gone to Libya to bring back his mother, and that he was captured and tortured, but escaped when NATO jets bombed the prison.

Of Abedi, an imam said, "He had hate in his eyes." Are we surprised? The Didsbury Mosque has invited some of the world's most notorious "hate preachers" to come and address the congregation.

This is going on in mosques throughout the country, and yet our political masters remain in total denial, because the truth is too much for them to face up to. They haven't the guts to say it how it is. We don't want to compound the problem and turn moderate Muslims against us, but we must address it with honesty and truth.

The American Dr. Sebastian Gorka is one of the world's leading experts in asymmetric warfare and counter-terrorism. In his wonderful book *Defeating Jihad: The Winnable War*, he reveals:

> In the plots we have intercepted, what we have learned about the division of labour in the jihadist enterprise is especially disturbing.

> Of the ISIS terrorists arrested or indicted inside America since the Islamic State was declared, just over half had sworn Bayat to the new caliph and were preparing to leave the country to fight for ISIS in the Middle East. Of the rest, 19% were acting as talent spotters or facilitators, like those management-level terrorists who vetted the young men and bought them their plane tickets to Turkey so they could cross into Syria to fight for the new empire. But, most shocking of all, 29% of the ISIS supporters caught or killed in the United States saw no need to go anywhere to become a jihadi. They had decided that the best way to serve the new caliphate and the new caliph, is to kill Americans here at home.

> [...] The Islamic State is much more than a regional insurgency threatening the nations of the Middle East or Africa. It is not a "junior varsity" terror team. The Islamic State is the twenty-first-century brand of global jihad, admired and emulated from Paris to Philadelphia

to San Bernardino. It is the centre of a new religious revolution that will continue to murder and devastate those it sees as the Infidel, expanding and inspiring mayhem here in America, unless it is stopped.

The situation in Great Britain and Europe is far worse. The density of population, the free movement of people, and the open-door policy, allowing the mass importation of undocumented migrants from war-torn Islamic countries, is playing Russian roulette with five bullets in the chamber. ISIS has openly declared that it intends to flood Europe with their warriors of the holy war. And yet, as the people of Europe scream and shout in protest, the European Union politicians continue to try and convince them that it is good for the economy. Civil unrest and civil disobedience are reaching epidemic proportions throughout the cities of Europe, and still the politicians and the media play it down. Although protest marches rage throughout the Continent, it is rarely reported on mainstream television. News of them has to come from witnesses and participants who post them on YouTube etc.

If anything, the establishment blames the disgruntled, indigenous population, branding them racists, Islam-phobic, fascists, and a whole string of descriptive words aimed at loading the burden of guilt upon the shoulders of the populace, who want nothing more than to preserve their own traditional culture, their nation's identity, and their democratic freedoms. Even the most hardnosed right-wing activist understands that carefully controlled immigration is essential for the growth of economies, but outright invasion is not!

In the Mediterranean Sea, the daily flotilla of boatloads of young, fit, able-bodied Arab and black African men and virtually no women or children, inflames the suspicions of motive. News reports describe them as "desperate" and "fleeing their war-torn homes." Why would they leave their elderly, their women, and their children behind to face the brutal consequences of war?

Those indigenous Europeans are rapidly losing their sense of compassion for their fellow man, knowing that there may be a more sinister objective lurking beneath the surface. The European Commission could solve this problem in an instant, by demanding that a United Nations military force be sent to the nations in question and that secure "Safe Zone Humanitarian Areas" be established, where fleeing civilians could receive UN-funded care and medication. Instead, the Commission has set up a taxi service to the European mainland, in order to reduce exploitation by the people traffickers.

Time and time again, Colonel Gaddafi of Libya had warned the West that a mass exodus by African migrants would flood into Europe if the West continued to destabilise the North African and Middle Eastern regions, and that included his own. He warned that if the European Union ever invited Turkey in as a member, it would be their Trojan horse to Islamic extremism. And yet, the West removed him in the most brutal fashion, on the pretext that he was an evil dictator who slaughtered his own people. It took the West forty-one years to decide just how evil he really was, before the decision was taken to assassinate him. In the spirit of fairness, I think we have to look at some facts. When Gaddafi came to power, Libya was a fairly poor, low infrastructure African country.

During his long tenure, he was responsible for creating the most sophisticated and largest irrigation system in the world, which he spread throughout the entire country: he made the desert smile. Any Libyan wishing to go into agriculture would be given farmland, seed, livestock, and agricultural training, entirely free. He built modern towns where all Libyans received free electricity. He modernised the road system and petrol was never charged to his people at more than 14 US cents per litre. Every pregnant woman received a bursary of $5,000 in order to help with the care of her and her new baby in the early days of the child's life.

Healthcare was entirely free to all his people.

When Gaddafi came to power, only around 20% of the population were literate. At the time of his death, 90% of the population could read and write, and 25% had attended university, achieving degrees in a wide variety of subjects. He distributed the nation's wealth to the people, which had been created by their vast sales from oil. This somehow just doesn't add up as qualifying him as the evil dictator we are led to believe. To me, he seems to compare very favourably against the likes of Mugabe, for example.

I feel the real reason for the removal of Gaddafi was far more sinister. Gaddafi was getting dangerously close to achieving his dream of freeing the entire continent of Africa from its perpetual debt to the Western banks and the planned world order of things. He wanted to introduce a single African gold currency, to be known as the African Dinar. The currency was based on that old adage that gold is what should back a currency's value, and quantitative easing, which is the mere printing of money on demand, is a worthless sham. Nowadays, the Western economies play that dangerous debt-ridden, money-printing game. Gaddafi wanted to have a gold-based central Bank of Africa and also to implement the introduction of an AMF (African Monetary Fund) which would mean that African countries would no longer require the services of the IMF (International Monetary Fund). If successful, it would have a devastating effect on the Euro and the US Dollar. Gaddafi's prophetic mutterings are proving to be true, and now the African migrant invasion of Europe is well underway.

Although nearly all the migrants are Muslim, not a single one of them is heading in the direction of an Islamic country, with the possible exception of Jordan, which is the most liberal and open-minded of the Islamic countries, and is therefore a potential for fundamentalism.

Saudi Arabia is refusing to take any of their fellow brethren in faith. However, the Saudis have promised to pay 100% of the funding to build 200 Sunni mosques throughout Germany in order to accommodate the mass influx of Islamic migrants heading their way.

Saudi Arabia is very aware that the writing is on the wall for their future prosperity and influence. Like the age of steam, which drove the Industrial Revolution, the requirement for oil is soon to become minimal as the petrol-driven combustion engine becomes obsolete. The rapid development of robotics, battery technology, solar energy, and the removal of the cash economy, only to be replaced by new forms of cyber money and cryptocurrency, will change the world immeasurably.

Most importantly of all, is the recent development of "Magma Energy Technology." That is the constant, inexhaustible, and entirely free source of energy which lies just below the surface of the earth, and is available to every country in the world. The next 50 years will astound us all.

The Saudis have a couple of ace cards to play, as far as securing their future power and influence in the world is concerned.

Firstly, they possess the two most precious holy Islamic centres of adoration, Mecca and Medina. And secondly, they are greatly increasing the Islamic control of the United Nations. They attempted to bring in a blasphemy law, making it illegal under international law to be critical of Islam, which they only just failed at doing by a handful of votes. Make no mistake, they will bide their time until they weaken Europe and get more control of some of the African countries; then they'll be back.

In areas of commerce, Saudi Arabia struggles, primarily because it is an oil-based economy with an absolute monarchist, feudal system of government. It relies heavily on the 7.5 million foreign workers to keep it all going. Official figures show that only 12% of all the Saudis who are of working age, have a job or are seeking employment. The problem lies in the fact that deep within the Middle Eastern mindset is a nomadic, Bedouin mentality. They lack the work ethic which is so much a part of Northern

European culture. The Saudis realise there is a need to diversify their economy and have tried to force companies to employ at least 30% young Saudi nationals. Employers complained bitterly about the lack of skills. Years of intense religious instruction had left young people ill-equipped to enter the job market.

The United Nations Arab Human Development Report says:

> Social and economic development is being inhibited because of poor education, a lack of personal freedom, corruption and the exclusion of women. There is also the obstacle of social resistance to certain types of employment.

Jobs in service and sales are considered totally unacceptable to Saudi citizens.

The armada of migrants swarming into Mediterranean Europe and heading straight for countries like Germany and Great Britain are primarily from that social and religious background. But, the European Commissioners assure everyone that they will be of enormous benefit to the prosperity of Europe.

What is actually happening is very much to the contrary. In Sweden, for example, police are struggling to cope with the crime increase perpetrated by the massive influx of youths, principally from Morocco, Afghanistan, and Syria. They mainly occupy the city shopping malls and are already involved in inter-gang drug warfare. Muggings, and gang rape of Swedish girls, are now a terrifying reality. Already there are 52 known no-go areas in Sweden where Muslim gangs patrol the streets telling the indigenous residents this is now a Muslim area and they are not welcome. In May 2017, the Swedish National Board of Forensic Medicine was called in to assist the Swedish Migration Agency, in order to ascertain the age group of migrants who entered the country as "unaccompanied children." In the first batch of 518, 442 were shown to be grown adults, of which 430 were men and 12 were women. A survey carried out by Swedish radio station showed that two years after receiving residence permits, only 3% of migrants were prepared to take classes to give them a basic education, which would be the minimum requirement for getting any kind of gainful employment. It would appear that immediately they are entitled to benefits, and thus they have little or no incentive to find work. This is not a biased observation: These are the inescapable facts.

A similar pattern of events is seen throughout most of the major cities of Europe and in Great Britain. Towns in England have experienced attacks on young women for being improperly dressed in an area close to a mosque and non-Muslim men have been attacked for drinking alcohol. The authorities continue to be economic with the truth and usually divert the argument by expounding the virtues of immigration.

"What would the National Health Service do without foreign nurses and doctors?" is a favourite response. The answer is very simple.

People who come here through the proper channels, and have something to offer, respect our laws and our customs, and have a genuine desire to integrate and enjoy the fruits of their labours, are usually made most welcome in nearly all Western democracies.

Those that just come to abuse the privileged lifestyle that the West has to offer them should be dealt with severely and without compromise.

Part of the problem is that there are no mandatory inclusion programmes set up to teach people about British culture, its customs, and its proud history.

They arrive and immediately move into a mini country within a country, and there they stay. Many live their entire lives without learning a word of English.

We now have a fragmented human geography within our own cities. There are areas where the police never enter; not for the fear of it, but because in densely populated Muslim communities, they are never called upon. Imams now deal with misdemeanours with their own parallel justice system; We know of at least 80 Sharia Courts already in Britain today. In addition to all of that, they also have their own preferred foreign banks, and financial centres, which have gravitated specifically to those areas. At a recent meeting in which I attended with a group of Pakistani businessmen, they were not in the least bit shy in telling me that they ship considerable amounts of unaccountable money out of the country via transfer companies, such as Western Union, on a daily basis. That should be a deeply sobering thought for our politicians to ponder.

There is nothing in place to make those people want to

become a part of their new home, and for them to strive toward citizenship for all the right reasons. The European Union's attempt to dilute and destroy the individuality of the separate countries of Europe is failing spectacularly. Forced multiculturalism doesn't work: It creates ghetto societies of deeply divided people.

Naturally, some cultures blend in quickly. The Jews, for example, many of which came to this country at the beginning of the twentieth century with nothing more than the clothes they stood up in, have contributed enormously. Their intelligence and their enterprise have enriched the country hugely. Jewish Reform has drifted many away from the rigid Jewish orthodoxy, and the modern world and the advances in science and education have steered many toward secularism. Reform, Orthodox, or Agnostic, it would be hard to find a people more proud to be British than the Jewish community.

The West's obsession with forcing democracy on the world is a misguided one. In certain cultures, benevolent dictatorship or an absolute monarchy works perfectly well, and in some cases it has survived for hundreds, if not thousands, of years. Democracy has to lead by the example of its success, not by sending out democratising missionaries.

Democracy never did sit comfortably upon the shoulders of Islam, for the obvious reason that state and the scriptures are as one. Thankfully, there are exceptions: Jordan and Egypt depend heavily on the tourist industry for their nations' survival and they do not share the same apocalyptic obsession as the fundamentalist jihadis, who have no respect for mankind's history before Muhammed in the seventh century AD. Baghdadi's ISIS troops would love to get close enough to the Sphinx if only to blow it up and destroy it completely.

Chapter 10

THE PROPAGANDA WAR: BEWARE OF SNAKE-OIL SALESMEN

It has to be said that since 9/11 we have witnessed over 19,000 acts of Islamic terrorism worldwide, all involving multiple deaths. The overwhelming majority of them have been Muslim against Muslim. The complexity of their conflict within Islam itself is multifaceted, as I'm sure that by now you realise only too well.

How do we solve this problem, and continue to retain our freedoms and our way of life without fear or hindrance?

At the risk of repeating myself, we have to start by examining ourselves, and putting a value on this way of life of ours. How much does it matter to us that our recent predecessors gave their lives defending it against German totalitarians who wanted to take it away from us? A follow-on from that came with the threat made by the Soviet Russians and their equally unpleasant form of totalitarianism.

We have to start by being honest, by telling the truth. By that, I mean we have to be able to openly name the enemy. We are not against Islam! We are not at war with the 1.5 billion Muslims who are peace-loving and want to get on with their lives and get on with us. We are against the 300 million Muslims who do want to kill us and impose their all-consuming apocalyptic ideology upon us.

We have to throw political correctness in the bin, where it belongs, and start with honesty. Political correctness disguises itself as being ever the champion for the aggrieved. In truth, it is mostly just a suppressor of the facts. An example was the London riots. Youths were filmed smashing shop windows, stealing computers and plasma screen televisions, and setting shops on fire. They were described as mindless yobs! As soon as it was realised that the vast majority were black, the media immediately back-tracked and blamed their deprived circumstances, lack of job opportunities, discrimination, poverty, poor housing. Many of those youths were brought up attending black Pentecostal churches; they were the sons of really good people. They knew full well what is right and what is wrong. No! They had become mindless yobs, and needed punishing to the fullest extent of the law.

We cannot allow political correctness to distort the truth, or pervert our response in securing the future of our way of life and our liberty.

It is remarkable that the jihadist fighters of this so-called holy war want to plunge the entire world back into the dark ages of the seventh century, and yet they have skilfully mastered the art of propaganda via the internet. On that front they are outmanoeuvring us and outsmarting us at every turn: Their recruitment videos are nothing short of brilliant. The reason for their amazing success is that the Western world has not joined in a collective counter-propaganda offensive. The internet is where this war is really being fought: We invented it! Why are they running rings round us? They have caught us on the hop and we still seem to be floundering without any kind of strategic communications plan. They have succeeded in appealing to the Islamic youth by making jihadism "really cool."

As a man with an advertising agency background, albeit a very long time ago, I realise the importance of branding the product. Our target market is Islam, and our objective is to separate the good Muslims from the bad Muslims. Therefore, we need to give the bad Muslims a product name that the good Muslims will want to disassociate themselves from. If the word "jihadi" is the only word that clearly defines bad Muslims, then it needs to be spun as "the true axis of evil." It needs to be associated with all that is bad in the world: derogatory, degrading, stupid, and backward-thinking, a club that only idiots want to join. An increased budget must be provided for the government's security services to come up with a massive counter-offensive internet propaganda programme, which must work closely with the Muslim community. If we are to win this war, then we have to divert the direction of it well away from Muslim vs. infidel, to good Muslim vs. bad jihadi Muslim and we must be there to assist the former in every way possible in order to win.

It will be impossible to win this conflict if we consider it a war against Islam in its entirety. If we do that, then the next generation of bad jihadi Muslims will be double in number to those of today, and the next, double again. The young are being brainwashed into believing that death is greater than life, and that the afterlife promises all the things that young men desire, such as virgins in paradise, and that is a very big hurdle to overcome.

They are being taught this nonsense by imams who grow old and live princely lives. If the cause is so perfect, why is it that suicide bombers are never old hate preachers? We must divide in order to conquer.

It is imperative that we stop our own non-Islamic people from continuing to refer to this conflict as a case of Muslims vs. Christians and, equally, good Muslims must be encouraged by the knowledge that Christians are on their side against their own internal enemy, but not against them.

Where do we start? We start by educating ourselves. You have to know your enemy, and you have to know precisely what makes him your enemy. I hope that in this book I have in some way shown the real problem Islam has within itself, and the seemingly insurmountable problem it faces. In the most diplomatic way possible, we must clearly show that we are 100% behind the Reformers: those that adhere to the early Meccan Quranic scriptures and not the intolerant brutal ones that belong to a very different, and less enlightened, society from the dark ages. The big problem is trying to weed out who is genuine and who is not. Those that want to deceive us are masters at it, and any that seek public office must expect to receive additional scrutiny. If they are genuine then they will understand our concerns and they will have to work harder to earn the nation's trust.

If we take, for example, the appointment of the London's Mayor, Sadiq Khan, who is a former lawyer and a Chairman of the Muslim Council of Britain's Legal Affairs Committee. As such, he defended the Muslim academic Dr. Yusuf al-Qaradawi. Khan did so despite the fact that this most learned of gentlemen seemed to hold some rather unpalatable views, such as his agreement with throwing homosexuals off mountaintops and the approval of men beating their wives. He also had some interesting opinions on suicide bombings, particularly in Israel. When questioned about martyrdom operations there, he is quoted as saying:

> God's justice: Allah Almighty is just; through his infinite wisdom he has given the weak a weapon the strong do not have, and that is, their ability to turn their bodies into bombs as Palestinians do.

Correct me if I'm wrong, but it would appear that London Mayor Khan didn't seem to think that al-Qaradawi's views were extreme. Khan's Legal Affairs Committee described al-Qaradawi as "a voice of reason and understanding" and Khan himself testified that "there is a consensus among Islamic scholars that Mr. al-Qaradawi is not the extremist that he is painted as being."

In our wonderful and free democracy, those we appoint to govern us, and with whom we entrust the control of our lives, have to be openly scrutinised, no matter who they are, and it is our duty to do so.

In Mayor Sadiq Khan's case, I wouldn't dream of suggesting that he is anything but honest, but somewhere, deep within the recess of my memory, the words of my dear, wise old grandmother come flooding back: "Point me out your company, and I'll tell you what you are!"

The average man on the street has little idea as to how difficult it is for our diplomatic and secret services to keep all the plates of diplomacy balanced and spinning in the air at the same time when dealing with the problem of radical Islam. Take the Muslim Brotherhood, for example. The Brotherhood was set up in Egypt in 1928, just after Ataturk got rid of the caliph. It now has separate and independent cells/chapters all over the world. Each has its own agenda, and therefore they are endlessly squabbling amongst themselves. The one thing they have in common is that they all believe that Sharia law is sacrosanct and Islam's dominance is its destiny.

In order for a government to officially categorise an organisation as a terrorist organisation, it has to be legally proven. With the Muslim Brotherhood, although it all shades under a single umbrella, some chapters are outright terrorists and some have political legitimacy. Therefore, under international law you would have to outlaw only the cell/chapter caught committing acts of terrorism. It's almost an impossible task, as in some countries they appear to be totally in tune with the democratic process and the political establishment. What I have difficulty with is that if they are all members of the same club, why are the rules so flexible as to allow some to be terrorists and some not to be?

Muslim Brotherhood members run for elections in democratic countries, and because of the strict Brotherhood rules of secrecy it is incredibly difficult to establish their true motives, or even if they are members of it at all. They have established parliamentary candidates in countries such as Kuwait and Jordan, even in Israel, and who knows where else. They can easily become the snake-oil salesmen of the type I mentioned earlier.

The integrity of our democracy has always been vulnerable, and it can easily be compromised and infiltrated by those whose ultimate aim is to corrupt and destroy it. It is for that very reason that we must be forever vigilant. In recent elections we have experienced a massive abuse of the postal voting system in places such as Birmingham, Bradford, Oldham, Burnley, and Tower Hamlets where the candidate was informing the constituents that if they didn't vote for him then Allah would not be merciful. At a by-election in Oldham during campaigning I witnessed voters, some who couldn't speak English, travelling to the mosque in order for the imam to fill out their postal voting papers. They quite innocently informed us of what they were doing.

I believe the time has come for the system to be completely overhauled. Postal votes should require a doctor's note. Ill health, disability, or being in the armed forces should be among the only reasons for requiring a postal vote, and not just because you couldn't be bothered going to the polling station. Prison inmates should forfeit their right to vote whilst serving their sentence.

Every voter should show valid identification at the polling booth when collecting their voting paper. I have to show photo ID for things far less important than voting, so that shouldn't be a problem. CCTV cameras should record each voter as they collect their paper. Those that have something to hide won't vote, and that's fine. Voting twice, as per the Cambridge University students who voted at home and in their university constituency, should be charged as criminals.

We didn't used to have this kind of problem, but times have changed, and now we do! We have to deal with it, because it can't continue for much longer if our precious democratic system is to survive intact.

So, what do we do next?

Firstly, our government needs a massive injection of political testosterone, followed by a high dosage of political-correctness-antibiotics. That will clear the system of any wobbly knees, ingratiating apologetic subservience, hand-wringing, and the constant nauseating feelings of unnecessary Islamic appeasement. This will strengthen the backbone of our politicians, restore integrity, and show a healthy return to an upright posture.

Nothing must be allowed to hinder the progress that we have made as a society in gaining our civil liberties and our people's rights. It has taken us far too long, and been far too hard-earned by those who fought and died before us. Female equality in Britain only started to come about in my grandmother's time, with the Suffragettes. I was a grown man by the time people who were homosexual were allowed to be free from the fear of prosecution in a criminal court.

All of that will disappear very rapidly if Islamic doctrine is allowed to creep into our legal system and into our government: Remember the instant transformation of Iran! Don't think for a second that it couldn't happen here: It could, and it will, unless we act with conviction and we are steadfast in valuing all that is precious to our way of life.

Sharia law must never be permitted in the West. There is but one law in Great Britain, and that is the law admissible in Her Majesty's Courts. Our system is the most just, and has long been proven to be so. You only have to look to the English-speaking democracies, and to those children of our former empire who have continued to celebrate our great legacy of Parliament and the rule of law, and there you will find, Stability, Prosperity, Democracy and Liberty. Never forget that under our democratic constitutional monarchist system the state exists to serve the people. Under a totalitarian Islamic State, the people exist to serve the state, and that, to us, is the most intolerable effrontery to our liberty.

The Islamic ideology is a boa constrictor: It will slowly asphyxiate the very breath of democracy from the lungs of each nation that unwittingly invites it into their home, for they will surely eventually have to surrender to its embrace.

We need to weed out the phoney Islamic charities that are so prevalent in our country today, and not be afraid to name, shame, dismantle, and confiscate their assets (which could help fund and assist genuine Muslim Reform groups).

We must outlaw all Wahhabi funding from Saudi Arabia for the building of mosques. This has absolutely nothing to do with spiritual needs, and everything to do with political and cultural subversion.

Universities and colleges throughout the Western world are easily seduced, and many already receive vast sums of money from Saudi Arabia on the pretext that it is there to promote a wider understanding of Islamic studies. It is no such thing: It has one purpose, and one purpose only!

Every single member of our police force, our armed services, the community workers, and the educators need to know about Islam and the threat Islamic extremism poses to our way of life. Education! Education! Education! is the key to it. If we show an interest, and we have sufficient knowledge to engage with Muslim people in meaningful conversations, then it will encourage the moderate Muslims to speak more openly with us. They will feel less fearful of expressing their moderate views in front of their own peers and imams when they know that every infidel knows the truth. It is fear and ignorance that drives it all underground and divides us, and we must bring it all out into the open. They can only continue to slowly undermine us as long as everyone is too afraid to speak out.

Chapter 11

WHERE DO WE GO FROM HERE?

───❦❧❦───

We do have a massive task ahead of us.

In a television interview immediately after the Manchester bombing, we watched the interviewer who was surrounded by a cross-section of the local Muslim community. One woman was there wearing a full-length black niqab and dark glasses. She was obviously only there to make a political statement. (Wearing the niqab has never been a legal or scriptural requirement on the Curry Mile in Rusholme! Nor anywhere else in Britain, for that matter.) During the interview, a middle-aged Muslim man was saying that they needed to interact a lot more with the non-Muslim community. In the background you could see several Muslim men shaking their heads in complete disapproval. The problem lies in the fact that they are totally indoctrinated from their childhood onwards with a hostility toward any outside influence. It has been fuelled by our disastrous foreign policy toward the Middle East for over many years.

The barrier to anything that may undermine absolute control by the imams and their continued promotion of an isolated Islamic tribalism is, for the average Muslim, maintained only by the fear of punishment or divine retribution.

The European Union's requirement for an open-door policy has created tight-knit ghetto societies throughout Great

Britain and Europe and penetrating them can now prove very difficult indeed.

If we try to force our way in, or force their community apart, then we will always be looked upon as the crusader trying to overpower Islam. It must come from within the Muslim community. We must engage with them and appear as merely their helpers in the struggle to modernise and destroy extremism within their ranks. At the same time we must never show any frailty or weakness in our own resolve to preserve our Western culture and values.

We are not on Arabian soil – they are on ours, and in this society the game is played by our rules. If it's not, then we will surely perish.

Our foreign policy with regards to handling the Middle East has been shambolic in the extreme. It's what comes with the election of gung-ho schoolboy politicians, the likes of Tony Blair and David Cameron, who always think they know best, and their vanity precludes them from accepting counsel from their betters, who have the advantage of the wisdom of age, knowledge, and experience. (On an American TV Show, David Cameron was unable to translate the meaning of Magna Carta! Unfortunately, he went to Eton. Had he have gone to Harrow, or Chorlton-cum-Hardy Primary School, he would have known the answer to that.)

Defeating ISIS and world jihadism is not going to be achieved by counter-insurgency attacks and by placing infidel boots on Islamic soil – unless they are invited, as in the case of Kuwait.

Read your history books: The answer always lies within their pages – which has just reminded me of the wise words of Rudyard Kipling, spoken at the height of the British Empire's involvement in the Middle East:

> At the end of the fight
> Is a tombstone white,
> With the name of the late deceased,
> And the epitaph drear,
> "A fool lies here,
> Who tried to hustle the East."

As soon as we send an invading force into Islamic territory, irrespective of it being against Sunnis or Shias, then millions of Muslims around the world think to themselves, the crusaders are back! And the 300 million who already hate us will have just increased recruitment to their ranks.

I believe the only time we need to employ our forces to the Islamic Middle East is as a "buddy force" to fight alongside those within the conflict who are most likely to give forward-thinking stable government, and who will ultimately serve our best interests in suppressing the spread of holy war jihadism.

Our superior strength in both expertise and high-tech military hardware should be used first and foremost in an advisory capacity and with special forces support.

Whenever it is required for our ground troops to be engaged in one of their wars, we need to have our soldiers appear as if they are on an equal footing to theirs, and victory in every skirmish must always be announced as theirs, with little or no mention of us. Let their history distort the facts; that's of little consequence to us.

Our goal is always the preservation of our own free, liberal culture of modernity and democracy; we must never lose sight of that.

When the day is done and the battle is won, we need to quietly leave without ceremony or pomp. Hopefully, we will leave them as grateful friends, having assisted them in moving one step closer to diluting their brutal seventh-century ideology and replacing it with a welcome Islamic Reformation that would be more in harmony with non-Muslim cultures around the world.

The answer to it all would under normal circumstances be trade! Nations that trade together have less reason for war. A healthy trade counter-balance has the ability to keep war at bay. However, as I have mentioned before: When dealing with the Middle East you are always faced with that nomadic Bedouin mentality that is so deeply ingrained within their psyche. The GDP created by the manufacturing of non-oil-related products for the entire Arabian Peninsula is less than that of Norway. Basically, they produce nothing that anybody wants, other than oil, and pretty soon we won't be wanting much of that.

We need to greatly expand our SAS and SBS special forces without compromising their standards of excellence. They are going to be needed a lot more in the future, as desk-top warfare technology increases and ground troops are required less. Special forces need to continue to be sent around the world to do what they have always done so brilliantly, and that is to assist in toppling rogue regimes from within, and helping to train useful insurgents. We need to redirect our foreign aid budget away from corrupt anti-Western Islamic countries like Pakistan and into helping our pro-Western Islamic friends like Jordan and Egypt. Squeeze out, isolate, and financially punish those that hate us. It's not difficult.

Our prime motivation, above all others, must be directed at clearing the threat from within our own shores.

As I write, a news item has just revealed that another sex grooming gang has been exposed. Again, it shows that thousands of young white English girls are being drugged and gang-raped around the country by these barbaric monsters.

The BBC newsreader says, "the men appear to be of Asian origin." This is an outrageous and shameful travesty of the facts and another example of the kind of political correctness that has to be stamped out once and for all.

I feel deeply saddened by this crass inaccurate reporting that may now affect the tens of thousands of Asian Sikhs, Buddhists, Christians, and Hindus who remain our neighbours and our friends.

The men responsible for these atrocities are "Asian Muslims!" They do it because it is laid down within the foundation stones of their religion, and they believe that that grants them the licence to satisfy their lust without fear of consequence. Can we please make that point perfectly clear from now on!

Can we defeat this entirely new kind of enemy from within our midst, who blatantly taunts us, and promises to eventually destroy our whole way of life? Yes we can!

But we will never furrow the fertile soil of home-grown jihadism, and begin to plant the seeds of hope, unless we are able to speak openly and honestly without fear of correction, prosecution, or retaliation. Those that govern us must be bold and forthright in taking the lead.

We need to be far less tolerant of Muslim community leaders in particular, who cunningly play at being the injured and the aggrieved whilst at the same time harbouring and promoting those who are the aggressors. They must be made to fear the full force of the law! With the direction things are presently progressing in, that is becoming less of an issue for them. They have been allowed to develop an arrogance and a lack of respect for our judiciary and our law enforcers, which has filtered down to the common man. For example, they refuse to stand for the judges in Her Majesty's Courts whilst being sentenced. This sends the clear message that they are above the law, and that they have an immunity merely because of their faith. No part of our judicial procedure must ever be violated. Mistaking tolerance for weakness is a deeply entrenched trait that goes back to the dawn of Islam. Give them an inch and they'll return to take a mile.

Our prisons are now a breeding ground for extremism, where inmates are being provided with Wahhabi versions of the Qur'an in addition to other seriously dangerous literature. Minority groups within our prisons today are being forced to convert to Islam by fear of death. Staff shortages have meant that the authorities are losing control and weak governance is allowing the fanatics to rule. This is one stinging nettle that must be grasped very firmly.

We must not be dismissive of the impact of this latest "Dawn of the Final Caliphate" which has been recently imposed upon the world by Abu Bakr al-Baghdadi. Even his death will barely slow the wheels of Islamic State's progress now that they have been set in motion around the world.

We have no choice but to help those within the Islamic world who are keen for a more tolerable Islamic Reform.

This war is winnable! And never be in any doubt of that.

It may be a slow, gradual process, and as time goes on we must never take our eye off the ball for a second. We must never allow our cultural and democratic way of life to be corrupted or compromised through an Islamic osmosis, if we are to survive.

We must prevent any further assault to the immune system of our Western values by first of all disarming the politically correct activists from within our own ranks.

We must identify the prominent true Islamic Reformers and give them every assistance possible in ridding Islam of its brutal and unacceptable martial identity and its desire to create an Islamic State.

We must gradually increase secularism through education, and broaden young minds in the direction of modern thinking, backed by scientific facts and not by blind faith or the brutality of ancient myth.

"As long as we live in this predatory world, War, will always be a fact in our lives. Cruel and evil though it may be, it has served as the engine of man's progress. It has extended the boundaries, and stretched the sinews of his inventiveness. Today, we are facing a new kind of enemy, whose agenda is the total assault on our freedom and our western values, and we must deal with him accordingly. In doing so, foremost in our minds, we must never falter, nor betray, the sacrifice of those before us who left us their precious legacy of liberty, and who gave their lives to free us from the tyranny of all of those totalitarians; whoever they may be."